MEXICO VIVO

A Spanish course on BBC Television

Course writer
Sue Baron
Ealing College of Higher Education

Editor
David Wilson

Researcher
Cristina Lago

Production Assistant
Elizabeth McDowell

MÉXICO VIVO

A BBC course in
Latin American Spanish

México Vivo is a Spanish course for post-beginners.

The course consists of

5 television programmes,

this course book and

an audio cassette.

Teachers' notes are also available.

This book accompanies the BBC Television series
México Vivo first broadcast on BBC1 in October 1990.

Producer:	David Wilson
Director:	Stephen Moss
Researchers:	Patricia de la Peña
	Cristina Lago
Production Assistants:	Elizabeth McDowell
	Fenella Sturt

Published to accompany a series of programmes prepared in consultation with the BBC Educational Broadcasting Council.

Published by BBC Books
A division of BBC Enterprises Ltd,
Woodlands, 80 Wood Lane, London W12 0TT

First published 1990

© The Author and BBC Enterprises Limited 1990

ISBN 0 563 21509 7

This book is set in 9/11pt Univers

Typeset by Ace Filmsetting Ltd, Frome, Somerset
Printed and bound in Great Britain by Richard Clay Ltd, Bungay
Cover printed by Richard Clay Ltd, Norwich

Contents

Mexico

Mexico is a rich mosaic of cultures, peoples and landscapes. It is the third largest country in Latin America, and four times the size of Spain. It shares a border with the U.S.A. almost 2,000 miles in length and has a coastline over 6,000 miles long.

Mexico's Pacific coast has attracted tourists for many years, but visitors are now exploring beyond Acapulco to discover the amazing variety of Mexico's landscapes. The north of the country is arid and in the south are tropical rain-forests. There are deep gorges and deserts, lakes and lagoons, pine forests and mangrove swamps. It is a rugged land, mostly mountainous, with the highest peaks in central Mexico: the snow-capped volcanoes of Ixtaccíhuatl (Sleeping Woman), Popocatépetl (Smoking Mountain) and Citlaltépetl (Starry Mountain), the highest at 18,700 feet.

Half the population of Mexico is under the age of fifteen, but it is a country with an ancient past still visible in the thousands of ruined temples and monuments. The first settlers here crossed from Asia to Alaska and down through North America. The earliest developed civilisation in Mexico was the Olmec, on the Gulf Coast, between 1200–300 B.C. Other civilisations followed, all of them highly organised and based around the great ceremonial centres whose remains can still be seen.

Mexico, showing major towns and other places mentioned in this book. Italics indicate locations featured in the television series

**Coahuila State, northern
Mexico**

**Tropical rain forest in the
southern state of Chiapas**

The Aztecs are perhaps the best-known of Mexico's pre-Hispanic peoples because their culture was the dominant one when the Spaniards arrived. Mexico was the first part of mainland America to be colonised by the Spanish. Their rule lasted three centuries, from 1521–1821, and left an indelible imprint on the culture and society. Spanish became the official language and Catholicism the official religion, though many of the old languages and beliefs persist to this day. Essentially, Mexico is a fusion of two worlds: three-quarters of the population are *mestizos* of mixed Spanish and Indian blood.

Mexico has had a very turbulent history. It was born out of violence. It struggled for many years to free itself from colonial rule. In the nineteenth century the new republic was vulnerable to foreign intervention. It lost over half its territory to the United States – California, New Mexico, Arizona, Texas. It was invaded by the French and had a foreign emperor, Maximilian. From 1876 until 1910 the dictatorship of Porfirio Díaz brought stability and the right conditions for commercial expansion and foreign investment. But repression, political stagnation and neglect of people's needs exploded in the great social upheaval of the Mexican Revolution of 1910 which cost a million and a half lives.

When the armed struggle ended, the struggle for political stability and economic reconstruction began. The myriad factions were united in 1929 under the single umbrella of the National Revolutionary Party which has dominated political life in Mexico until today (it is now called the PRI, the Institutional Revolutionary Party). Mexico solved the problem of army coups, regionalist factions and personal dictatorship. It has been the most stable country in Latin America for fifty years. It faces many great challenges: the pressures of the massive foreign debt, the opening-up of the political system, a flexible response to the people's demand for greater democracy and social justice and a young, rapidly-increasing population who will take the country into the twenty-first century.

The course

México Vivo is an intermediate stage for beginners between **España Viva** and **Paso Doble**. It builds on the vocabulary and basic grammar points presented in **España Viva** and adds a lot of useful new words and phrases, and a little more grammar.

México Vivo teaches the Spanish you need to cope with a variety of practical situations, whether on holiday or business: making travel arrangements, changing money, hiring a car, making phone calls, getting things repaired. It also teaches language useful for expressing opinions and describing things. The course is based on dialogues and interviews specially filmed in Mexico.

México Vivo also introduces the sights and sounds of Mexico, which has more Spanish speakers than any other nation in the world. It is a huge country with a rich variety of landscapes, traditions and cultures. The course offers glimpses into this land which tourism is now beginning to open up.

THE TELEVISION PROGRAMMES

Each of the five programmes contains a number of dialogues or interviews showing the language to be learnt in its context. These are the basis of the course. There are also two or three short film reports, *reportajes*, showing different aspects of life in Mexico – from coral reefs to cattle ranching and from ancient monuments to Indian crafts. These reports are all in Spanish, but beginners are not expected to understand much: for this reason, English sub-titles are provided. But just listening to the speech is a useful way of attuning to the sounds of Spanish.

The programmes were filmed in different and contrasting locations to give some idea of the diversity of Mexico and the exciting possibilities it offers to the traveller. As well as Mexico City, the series shows Morelos and Oaxaca to the south of the capital, Tabasco on the Gulf of Mexico, northern Chiapas and Quintana Roo on the Caribbean coast. The interviewer is Patricia de la Peña.

THE BOOK

It is an essential part of the course and can be used on its own when the television programmes are not being shown.

The five main chapters of the book correspond to the television programmes. Each chapter consists of:

En Directo

The text of the dialogues recorded in Mexico. New vocabulary is translated alongside the text and key phrases are highlighted in boxes. Specific Mexican expressions or words are indicated by the abbreviation (Mex). (Mex) after a Spanish word indicates it is rarely or never used in Spain; (Mex) after a translation indicates this meaning rarely or never applies in Spain. All words, including those already taught in **España Viva**, are listed in the **Vocabulary** at the back of the book. At the end of each dialogue is a **Spot-check** in English to see if you have understood: answers are given in the **Key** section at the back of the book. You will find occasional notes on idioms below the text.

Vocabulario

includes the key words appearing in **En Directo**, with some additional vocabulary which you will find useful in the same context. Any Mexicanisms are listed with the peninsular Spanish equivalents on page 97.

Así se dice

summarises the key structures of the chapter.

Notas de lengua

explains points of grammar and idiom.

Lecturas

are summaries in Spanish of the television *reportajes* and provide background information to the chapter. They contain a good deal of new vocabulary (used in the television programmes): beginners should not expect to understand everything. However, they offer an opportunity to tackle short passages of Spanish prose if you are ambitious. They can also be used as a way of preparing for the television programme to increase understanding of the Spanish. If you want to test your comprehension, there are questions in English; you can check your answers against the literal translation at the end of the book.

Extra

This section is an optional one for those who want to extend their vocabulary beyond the basics taught in **En Directo**. It contains extra dialogues dealing with everyday situations, with an emphasis on colloquial, social language. Unfamiliar words and phrases are translated and there are a couple of true/false questions in Spanish if you want to check how well you have understood: the answers appear in the **Key** section. These dialogues can be heard on the audio cassette.

México Vivo

A series of short articles in English to provide you with general background information for the chapter and introduce you to aspects of Mexico's history, cultural life and present-day issues. A book-list is provided at the end of the book if you wish to explore the subjects further.

Prácticas

In these exercises you can practise the points of grammar and idiom set out in the chapter. A key at the back of the book provides the answers. The final exercise of each **Prácticas** section, *¿Conoce usted México?*, is not exactly 'Mastermind' but a series of questions about everything in the chapter for you to ponder on (not too seriously).

The reference section at the back of the book contains:

- an outline of the main differences between the Spanish of Mexico and that spoken in Spain, including differences in words in the **Vocabulario** sections
- a reading list
- a summary of the main grammar points taught in **España Viva**, on which **México Vivo** is based
- a summary of the main grammar points taught in **México Vivo**
- translations of the **Lecturas**
- **Key**: answers to **Spot-checks**, **¿Verdad?** and **Prácticas**
- **Word groups**: additional useful words connected with some of the topics covered in the book
- **Vocabulary**: a translation of all Spanish words in the chapters except those in the **Lecturas**.

THE AUDIO CASSETTE

This contains recordings of all the **En Directo** and **Extra** dialogues, together with pronunciation practice and exercises.

THE TEACHERS' NOTES

A booklet intended mainly for teachers using the course at adult education classes. It offers suggestions for the use of the course in the classroom. It also contains a transcript of the television *reportajes* to assist teachers wishing to make use of the resource material. The notes are available by sending a cheque or postal order for £3.20, payable to BBC Education, to: MEXICO VIVO, BBC Education, BBC White City, 201 Wood Lane, London W12 7TS.

How to use the book

Before you start, you may want to check up on the language taught in **España Viva**, which is the starting point of this course. A summary of the main grammar points is provided in **Grammar revision: España Viva** (page 88).

In the main five chapters, read the **En Directo** dialogues, learn the key structures and new vocabulary, study the **Notas de Lengua** and then do the **Prácticas** to see how much you have absorbed. Obviously this won't be done in one sitting! Work at a pace you find comfortable, come to grips with the new material *poco a poco*. You will find that there are relatively few new key structures in each chapter and these can be learned fairly quickly; the vocabulary is more abundant and therefore 'chop it up' into small blocks. Study the **En Directo** dialogues before the programmes so you can concentrate on listening to the spoken language. If you feel you can cope, look at the **Lecturas** and then watch the *reportajes* without trying to follow the text at the same time: see how much language you can recognise. If you take the **Lecturas** just as reading material, see how much you can understand before turning to the translation. After you have digested the 'main' part of the chapter, you can turn to the **Extra** dialogues if you wish: see what phrases you recognise and learn any new vocabulary which you think could be useful for you.

Spanish in Latin America

Spanish is spoken in nearly all Latin American countries except Brazil, making it third in the world in terms of the number of mother-tongue speakers. The Spaniards introduced it in 1492 and at the height of their colonial power the language was spoken all the way from the Antilles to Tierra del Fuego and north into what is now the United States, as witnessed by such place names as San Francisco, Los Angeles, Nevada, Colorado.

The differences between the Spanish of Latin America and that of Spain are no more than the differences between one part of the English-speaking world and another. In fact, it is often forgotten how many variations of language exist within Spain itself. But despite the differences of accent, idiom and vocabulary, people understand each other.

The differences in Spanish arose for various reasons: because of the different environment – flora, fauna etc., the influence of Indian languages and the period when the countries were conquered and colonised. What distinguishes Mexican Spanish from that of other countries is principally the enormous number of words of Nahuatl origin. Nahuatl was the language of the Aztec empire and is still spoken today. Words like *nopal* (type of cactus), *guajolote* (turkey), *mecate* (rope), *huarache* (sandals), *elote* (sweet corn) are part and parcel of everyday language in Mexico.

Not all native words remain local to the place which produced them: some have become much more widely used. When the Spanish first arrived in the West Indies, they discovered a number of things they had never seen before and for which they adopted native words: *tabaco, iguana, huracán, batata, hamaca, canoa*. Moving on to Mexico, they adopted other words for yet more new things: *aguacate* (avocado), *chile, tomate, chocolate*. From Spanish, many of these words have entered English and other languages.

1 La ciudad más grande del mundo

> En tanto que permanezca el mundo
> no acabará la fama y la gloria de
> México–Tenochtitlán
>
> Memorias de Culhuacán

GETTING AROUND
ASKING FOR INFORMATION

EN DIRECTO

1 At Mexico City airport, Alfonso Flores asks at the
information desk about transport to the city centre.

Alfonso:	Buenos días, señorita.		
Empleada:	Buenos días. A sus órdenes.	**a sus**	*Yes, may I help*
Alfonso:	¿Me puede decir cómo llego al centro, por favor?	**órdenes** (Mex)	*you?*
Empleada:	Claro que sí. Puede tomar un taxi o si no trae	**si no trae**	*if you haven't*
	equipaje puede tomar el metro.	**equipaje**	*any luggage*
Alfonso:	¿Y no hay camiones?	**camiones**	*buses*
Empleada:	No, no hay.		
Alfonso:	Entonces, ¿dónde puedo tomar un taxi?		
Empleada:	Saliendo a su derecha está la taquilla de taxis. Ahí	**saliendo**	*as you go out*
	tiene que comprar su boleto.	**taquilla**	*ticket-kiosk*
Alfonso:	¿Y cuánto cuesta el boleto?	**ahí**	*there*
Empleada:	Depende de la zona. Al centro son más o menos diez	**tiene que**	*you have to buy*
	mil pesos.	**comprar**	
Alfonso:	Bien, gracias.	**boleto**	*ticket*
Empleada:	Para servirle.	**depende de**	*it depends on*

● **Spot-check 1** 1 Why can't Alfonso go by Underground?
  2 Where is the taxi ticket-booth?

**La Avenida de los Insurgentes looking south. In
the background is the extinct volcano of El Ajusco**

> *To ask for information:*
> **¿me puede decir . . .?**
> *To ask how to get somewhere:*
> **¿cómo llego a . . .?**

A sus órdenes

Mexicans tend to be polite and fairly formal in speech. When using a greeting like *Buenos días/ muy buenos días* etc., it is common to add *señor, señora* etc., or titles (if known) such as *Doctor(a), Licenciado/a* (strictly speaking a lawyer but frequently used for anyone with a university degree).

You will often hear the expression *a sus órdenes* in Mexico meaning either 'can I help you?' or 'at your service'. *¿En qué puedo servirle?* is also used, as in Spain.

When giving thanks, one often adds *muy amable/ muy amable de su parte*, to which the reply may be *de nada/para servirle* which loosely mean 'don't mention it'. You may also hear *¡qué le vaya bien!* which means something like 'have a nice day'.

Double-take

Tomar is always used in Mexico for catching/taking/ getting buses, trains etc. Although *coger* is often used with this meaning in Spain, it has rude connotations in Mexico and should be avoided.

If you have to change trains/buses etc. the phrase is *cambiar de: ¿tengo que cambiar de tren?* 'do I have to change trains?'. In the Mexico City metro, the sign CORRESPONDENCIA indicates a connection.

2 Alfonso goes to the kiosk selling tickets for taxis.

Alfonso:	Buenos días. Un boleto para el Hotel Reforma en la calle de París, por favor.
Empleado:	Está en la colonia Cuauhtémoc, ¿verdad?
Alfonso:	Sí, ahí está.
Empleado:	Es zona cuatro. Le cuesta diez mil quinientos.
Alfonso:	Aquí tiene. (*He pays and takes his ticket.*) Bien, gracias.
Empleado:	Para servirle.

colonia   *district*

● **Spot-check 2** 1 Which district is the hotel in?
2 How much does Alfonso pay for the ticket?

Here and there
ahí, allí, allá Spanish uses two words to mean
'there': *ahí* tends to refer to something quite close;
allí to something further away. You will also hear *allá*,
which means a long way away: *allá en España*. A
classic of the golden age of Mexican cinema is *Allá
en el Rancho Grande*.

Aquí, acá As well as *aquí, acá* is used to mean
'here':
¿cuándo vienes para acá? When are you coming over
here?
¡vente para acá! come here!
Acá and *allá* are widely used in Mexico.

3 Patricia de la Peña hails a taxi to go to la Plaza de las
Tres Culturas, which represents the three stages of
Mexico's history: pre-Colombian, colonial and
modern.

Patricia:	Buenas tardes, señor. Quiero ir a la Plaza de las Tres Culturas. ¿Cuánto me cobra?
Taxista:	Ah. Está en la colonia Tlatelolco, ¿no?
Patricia:	Sí, en la Avenida Lázaro Cárdenas, entre Eulalio Guzmán y Manuel González.
Taxista:	Entonces son seis mil pesos.
Patricia:	Está bien. (*The taxi approaches the Plaza.*) ¿Me puede dejar en la esquina donde está el semáforo, por favor?

taxista *taxi-driver*
entre *between*
pesos *units of Mexican currency*
dejar *leave*
esquina *corner*

● **Spot-check 3** Where does Patricia want the taxi driver to
leave her?

To ask how much you'll be charged:
¿cuánto me cobra?
and to agree to the price:
está bien

Cornered
In Spanish there are two words for 'corner'. *Esquina* is the sort you can turn at, *dar vuelta en*, wait on, *esperar en*, or go round, *doblar*. The corner of a room is *el rincón*, the sort you might ask to sit in at a restaurant.

Street names
Streets are often referred to in Spanish without saying *calle*, *avenida* etc. So Eulalio Guzmán means la calle de Eulalio Guzmán. And la Avenida de los Insurgentes, the longest urban street in the world, is known just as Insurgentes.

4   A visitor to Mexico City wants to find out the way to the Templo Mayor, a major Aztec archaeological site.

Juan Pablo:	¡Disculpe! ¿Para ir al Templo Mayor?		
Transeúnte:	El Templo Mayor . . . Después de la siguiente glorieta, da vuelta a la derecha en Avenida Juárez y se sigue todo derecho hasta llegar al Zócalo. Allí está el Templo Mayor, detrás de la catedral.	**transeúnte** **siguiente** **glorieta** **da vuelta** **detrás de**	*passer-by* *next* *roundabout* *you turn* *behind*
Juan Pablo:	¿Está muy lejos, no?		
Transeúnte:	Pues sí. Bastante lejos . . . como a veinte minutos a pie.	**como a** **a pie**	*about* *on foot*
Juan Pablo:	¿Hay una estación de metro por aquí?	**metro**	*underground railway*
Transeúnte:	Sí, a dos o tres cuadras hay una.	**cuadras**	*blocks* (Mex)
Juan Pablo:	Gracias. Muy amable.		
Transeúnte:	De nada.		

● **Spot-check 4**   1 Which way should Juan Pablo turn after the roundabout?
2 How long does it take to walk to the Templo Mayor?

To approach a passer-by:
¡disculpe!
or **¡discúlpeme!**

To ask the way:
¿para ir a . . .?

Excavations at the Aztec Templo Mayor; with the Cathedral and Sacristy in the background

VOCABULARIO

el metro	underground
el camión	bus (Mex)
la taquilla	ticket-desk
el sitio	taxi-rank (Mex)
el boleto	ticket (Mex)
la glorieta	roundabout
la cuadra	block (Mex)
la colonia	district (Mex)
la esquina	corner
la maleta	suit-case
traer	to bring/carry
tomar	to take/catch
llevar	to take/carry
bajar(se) de	to get off
subir(se) a	to get into/on
dar vuelta en	to turn at
cobrar	to charge

dejar	to leave
ir a pie	to walk
poder	to be able to
esperar	to wait for
ayudar	to help
cambiar (de)	to change (trains, buses etc.)
detrás de	behind
delante de	in front of
al lado de	next to
enfrente de	in front of, opposite

ASI SE DICE

To approach a passer-by:
¡disculpe! or ¡discúlpeme!
¡perdón! or ¡perdóneme!
And to thank them:
muy amable

To ask how to get somewhere:
¿para ir a . . .?
¿cómo | llego | a . . .?
| voy |

To ask if someone can do something for you:
¿me puede | decir?
| dejar?
| ayudar?
| llevar?

To find out how much you'll be charged:
¿Cuánto me cobra?
And to agree to the price:
está bien
de acuerdo

To ask to be taken somewhere:
quiero ir a . . .   I want to go to . . .
¿me lleva a . . .?   will you take me to . . .?

NOTAS DE LENGUA

me, him, her . . .

In phrases like *¿me lleva?*, *¿me puede decir?*, *me* is
an object pronoun ('me' in English). There are direct
objects: 'I like **her**', 'we ate **it**', 'they took **us**', and
indirect objects: 'I gave it **to her**', 'they wrote **to us**',
'he spoke **to me**'.

In Spanish, the object pronouns are:

me   me, to me
te   you, to you (informal, singular)
le   you, to you (formal, singular); him, to him; her,
          to her
la   you (feminine, formal, singular); her; it
          (feminine)
lo   you (masculine, formal, singular); him; it
          (masculine)
nos   us, to us
os   you, to you (informal, plural)
les   you, to you (formal, plural); them, to them
las   them (feminine)
los   them (masculine)

Notice the position of object pronouns, which usually
come before the verb in Spanish:
*¿**me** lleva?*   will you take **me**?
***lo** compro*   I'll buy **it**

In phrases like *¿me puede ayudar?*, the pronoun can
either come before the first (modal) verb or after, and
attached to, the second verb (in the infinitive):
*¿puede ayudar**me**?*
Another example:
lo** quiero comprar* or *quiero comprar**lo

There are two differences between Mexican and
peninsular Spanish usage:

a The *os* form is not used in Mexico because the
vosotros form of address is not used; *ustedes*
refers to 'you', both 'familiar' and 'formal', in the
plural.
b In some parts of Spain *le* is used to mean 'him,
her' as well as 'to him, to her' and *les* is used to
mean 'them' as well as 'to them' when referring to
people; *lo, la, los, las* are only used when referring
to objects.
Compare the Mexican and Spanish ways of saying
'I'm seeing him tomorrow':
lo veo mañana (Mexico)
le veo mañana (Spain)

Being emphatic

When you want to emphasise the pronoun as in '**We**
don't like tacos', 'Do **you** like tacos?', the Spanish is:
a nosotros, no nos gustan los tacos
a ustedes, ¿les gustan los tacos?
Note that personal pronouns when used
emphatically like this are different from the subject
pronouns in the first and second person singular:
*a **mí**, me gustan los tacos*
*a **ti**, ¿te gustan los tacos?*

'Personal' a

When a person is the object of a verb, it must be
preceded by *a*:
    *veo **a** Juan*   I see Juan
    *conozco **a** ellos*   I know them
    *acompaño **al** director*   I'm going with the director

The 'personal' *a* is also used before animals or other
animate objects; but it doesn't usually precede an
inanimate object:
    *veo **el** libro*
    *conoce **la** ciudad*

The 'personal' a has no translatable meaning, unlike the a which precedes an indirect object as in:
escribo a Juan   I'm writing **to** Juan

LECTURAS

Ciudad de México, ayer y hoy

A dos mil metros de altura, la ciudad de México se encuentra rodeada de montañas y volcanes.

Su emplazamiento fue elegido por los aztecas, que fundaron la ciudad en 1325, llamándola Tenochtitlán. Fue la capital de su imperio hasta la conquista de los españoles en 1521.

Los españoles destruyeron el imperio azteca. Sobre las ruinas de Tenochtitlán, construyeron una nueva ciudad.

Hoy en día, todavía puede apreciarse la huella del pasado azteca y español de esta gran capital, la más poblada del mundo con 19 millones de habitantes. Es una ciudad industrial, donde vive un cuarto de la población del país. Para sus habitantes, la contaminación y el tráfico son dos de los problemas más graves de la capital. Pero a pesar de los problemas, los chilangos sienten un gran apego por su ciudad.

1 What is Mexico City surrounded by?
2 Who chose the site for the city?
3 What problems is Mexico City facing today?

Cristina Pacheco

La ciudad de los milagros

Muchos de los millones de habitantes de la ciudad de México son emigrantes, que un día abandonaron el campo por la capital. Una de ellos es Cristina Pacheco, una popular periodista y escritora.

Para Cristina, la calle más larga del mundo – la Avenida de los Insurgentes – es una buena muestra de la complejidad de la ciudad.

En su parte norte, la avenida llega hasta el humilde barrio de los Indios Verdes, donde viven miles de inmigrantes, que llegaron aquí con la esperanza de encontrar una vida mejor. Como dice Cristina,

'Vienen en busca de un sueño, de una fantasía, de una posibilidad'.

Indios Verdes muestra una de las caras de la ciudad. Pero veinte kilómetros hacia el sur, Insurgentes cruza una zona bien distinta: el próspero centro. Esta fue una parte de la capital muy afectada por el terremoto de 1985, siempre presente en la memoria de los mexicanos: 'Es terrible ver que la ciudad donde creciste, donde está lo que más amas, de pronto se deshace'.

Más hacia el sur de Insurgentes se encuentran los tranquilos y exclusivos barrios residenciales, donde no existe la miseria.

Sin duda una ciudad de contrastes, Cristina define a México como 'una ciudad de los milagros', afirmando que 'La ciudad más poblada del mundo es también la más generosa'.

1 What is Cristina Pacheco's profession?
2 Why do so many people come to live in Mexico City?
3 What happened to the city centre in 1985?
4 Why does Cristina Pacheco think that Insurgentes reflects the complexity of the city?

EXTRA

A Beatriz is in Mexico City for a few days and phones up a friend to find out the way to the University.

Beatriz:	Oye, Mario – mañana tengo que ir a la Universidad. Voy a tardar menos tiempo en metro que en camión, ¿no?	**tardar**	*to take (time)*
Mario:	¡Claro!		
Beatriz:	¿Qué hago entonces?		
Mario:	Tomas la línea 1 en Insurgentes – dirección Pantitlán.		
Beatriz:	¿Mande?	**¿mande?**	*pardon? (Mex)*
Mario:	Pantitlán . . . y te bajas en Balderas para tomar la línea 3 dirección Universidad.		
Beatriz:	¿Y no me voy a perder?	**¿no me voy a perder?**	*won't I get lost?*
Mario:	Ay, ¡cómo eres! Es muy fácil. Para cambiar buscas 'Correspondencia' y tomas el otro tren. Hay dos estaciones para la Universidad. ¿A qué parte vas a ir?	**buscas**	*you look for*
Beatriz:	A la Facultad de Filosofía y Letras.		
Mario:	Entonces tienes que bajarte en Copilco. La Facultad está allí cerquita.	**Facultad**	*Faculty*
Beatriz:	¡Ay! Muchas gracias. En la nochecita te hablo.		
Mario:	De acuerdo.		

¿Verdad? Are these statements true or false?
1 Beatriz tiene que tomar el metro en Pantitlán.
2 La Facultad está cerca de la estación de metro.

B Josefina has just arrived in Mexico City and gets talking to the taxi driver.

Taxista:	Buenas tardes. ¿A dónde quiere ir, señorita?		
Josefina:	A la colonia del Valle. A Búfalo con Félix Cuevas.		
Taxista:	Muy bien. ¿Le pongo la maleta en la cajuela?	**cajuela** (Mex)	*boot (of car)*

Josefina:	No, gracias. No pesa nada.	**no pesa nada**	*it doesn't weigh anything*
Taxista:	¿Usted no es de aquí, señorita?		
Josefina:	No, soy de Veracruz. Vengo a la boda de una prima.	**boda**	*wedding*
Taxista:	¡Ah, qué bonito! ¿Se va a casar con un chilango?	**prima**	*cousin (female)*
Josefina:	Sí, es un muchacho muy simpático. Es médico.	**chilango (Mex)**	*someone from Mexico City*
Taxista:	Pues, también ustedes los veracruzanos tienen fama de ser muy simpáticos.	**muchacho**	*boy*
Josefina:	Sí, es cierto. Somos muy alegres. ¿Y usted es del D.F.?	**tienen fama de**	*have the reputation of*
Taxista:	No, soy de un pueblito de Michoacán.	**es cierto**	*that's true*
Josefina:	Ah, Michoacán me encanta. Es un estado precioso. ¿Y no extraña su tierra?	**alegres**	*cheerful*
		precioso	*beautiful*
Taxista:	Sí, pero llevo diez años trabajando en el D.F. y mis hijos ya están en la escuela.	**¿no extraña su tierra?**	*don't you miss your home? (Mex)*
Josefina:	Quizás algún día regrese a su tierra . . .	**llevo diez años trabajando**	*I've been working for ten years*
Taxista:	Quién sabe, señorita . . . ¡Pues ojalá!		
		quizás algún día regrese	*perhaps one day you'll go back*
		¡ojalá!	*let's hope so!*

¿Verdad?
1 Josefina prefiere que el taxista ponga la maleta en la cajuela.
2 El taxista piensa que los veracruzanos son muy amables.

C A tourist asks the hotel receptionist about trips to Teotihuacán.

Turista:	Buenos días, señorita. ¿Nos podría decir cuál es la mejor manera de ir a las Pirámides?	**¿podría . . . ?**	*could you . . . ?*
Recepcionista:	¿Cuántas personas son?	**les conviene**	*it would be better*
Turista:	Cuatro.		
Recepcionista:	Entonces les conviene ir en taxi.	**¿no nos va a salir . . . ?**	*won't it work out*
Turista:	¿Pero no nos va a salir muy caro?		
Recepcionista:	No, hay un precio fijo. Son treinta mil pesos por hora. Quizás para dos personas sería más económico tomar un 'tour' pero como ustedes son cuatro . . .	**precio fijo**	*fixed price*
		quizás	*perhaps*
		sería	*it would be*
Turista:	¿Y cuánto tiempo se tarda en llegar?	**¿cuánto tiempo se tarda en llegar?**	*how long does it take to get there?*
Recepcionista:	Una hora aproximadamente.		
Turista:	¿Y se puede comer allá?		
Recepcionista:	Claro que sí. Hay un buen restorán. Además, el taxista puede esperar y regresarlos a México.	**el restorán = el restaurante**	
		regresarlos	*bring you back*
Turista:	¡Estupendo! ¿Tenemos que llamar al sitio?	**frente a = enfrente de**	
Recepcionista:	No, los taxis están ahí, frente al hotel.		
Turista:	Muchas gracias.		
Recepcionista:	De nada. ¡Qué les vaya muy bien!		

¿Verdad?
1 Cada turista tiene que pagar 30.000 pesos para ir en taxi a las Pirámides.
2 No es necesario llamar al sitio para un taxi.

MEXICO VIVO

The Aztecs

The Aztecs (or *Mexicas*) were a nomadic tribe from the north who moved into the Valley of Mexico in the thirteenth century. According to legend, their god Huitzilopochtli told them to build a city in the place where they saw an eagle holding a snake in its beak and perched on a cactus growing from a rock. And so Tenochtitlán was founded in 1325 on an island in the middle of lake Texcoco. The eagle, snake and cactus have become the national emblem of Mexico.

Tenochtitlán was to become a magnificent city with canals and floating gardens, linked to the shores of the lake by causeways. From their capital, the Aztecs ruled over an ever-expanding empire, exacting tributes and human sacrifices from the tribes they had subjugated.

The story of the Spanish conquest is an epic one. A small, tired army under Hernán Cortes was no match for the Aztecs. But with the help of tribes who resented Aztec domination the Spanish finally gained control of Tenochtitlán in 1521 and destroyed it in order to build their own capital.

Very little remains of the Aztec civilisation apart from their language, Nahuatl, which is still spoken by some three million people. It is difficult to imagine the grandeur of their civilisation, but some idea of the scale of la Gran Tenochtitlán can be gained from the remains of their most important ceremonial centre, the Templo Mayor, discovered in 1978 by electricians laying a cable in Mexico City's main square.

La Ciudad de México

Mexico City, officially *la Ciudad de México*, is usually referred to just as *México* or *el Distrito Federal – el D.F.* for short. The capital has mushroomed over the past three decades with the exodus of people from the country. Today, it has become the most densely populated conurbation in the world with 11 million people in the city itself and 8 million more in the built-up area around it.

Mexico City is the hub of a highly centralised nation. 22% of the country's population lives in the capital; half the nation's industry is based here and almost half its commerce; the city's medical, educational and cultural facilities also represent almost half the national totals.

This centralisation is a feature of Mexican society which some observers trace back to the Aztecs. It has created problems on a scale to match the city's size, and the Government is determined to change it.

Mexico City for the visitor

The first impression of Mexico City can be overwhelming. The sheer size of the capital plus the initial effects of the altitude can be breathtaking! Yet no-one can fail to be impressed by the city's vitality or fascinated by its contrasts. Any visit should start from the Zócalo – second in size only to Red Square, Moscow – with its massive cathedral built by the Spaniards from Aztec stones on one side, the National Palace – decorated with Rivera murals – on another, and in between, the excavations of the Aztec Templo Mayor.

The city boasts the world's largest urban park – Chapultepec ('grass-hopper hill'), the magnificent Museo de Antropología and a splendid theatre/concert hall, el Palacio de Bellas Artes, built of Italian marble and containing a superb Tiffany glass curtain.

Boats for hire on the canals of Xochimilco

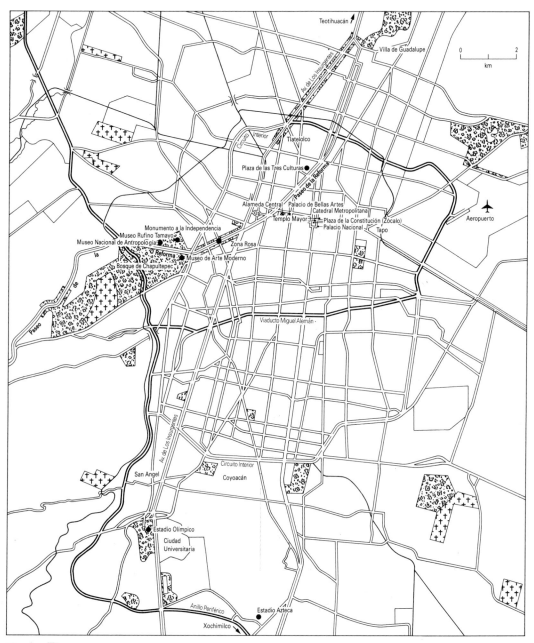

Mexico City

In contrast, one can wander through the cobbled streets and tree-lined squares of San Angel and Coyoacán, formerly independent villages, which have been swallowed up by *el monstruo* but retain their individual charm and tranquillity. In the far south of the City, the canals of Xochimilco are a favourite Sunday outing. Sundays are also a good time to visit the spiritual focus of Mexico, the Basilica of Nuestra Señora de Guadalupe, patron saint of Mexico.

An hour's drive away from the city centre is one of the most important and impressive archaeological sites of Mexico – Teotihuacán, or las Pirámides, as it's also known. The most famous feature is a vast ceremonial avenue, la Calzada de los Muertos, lined with archaeological remains including the monumental pyramids of the Sun and the Moon.

What's in a name?

All over Mexico, streets and squares are named after national heroes, important historical events, former presidents and certain articles of the Constitution – for example, Juárez, Madero, Reforma, Artículo 123,

16 de septiembre. Mexico City boasts the longest urban street in the world, named after the fighters for independence from Spain, la Avenida de los Insurgentes. The country's roots can be seen in the wealth of indigenous place names: Cuauhtémoc, Xicotencatl, Xochimilco, Chapultepec.

Public transport in Mexico City

The underground system – *el metro* – is fast, clean and cheap, but should be avoided during rush-hours (7–9 am, 1–3 and 7–8 pm) unless you want first-hand experience of *la explosión demográfica*. There is only one price for tickets. If you prefer to travel above ground, there are buses – *camiones* – and minibuses – *colectivos* or *peseros* – which ply all the major routes and charge a set fare. They are a less crowded mode of transport than buses and charge more.

Taxi!

There are three types of taxi: the *turismo* – luxury saloons found outside the more expensive hotels, which have their own fare-scale; the orange *sitio*

La Gran Tenochtitlán; Diego Rivera's mural in the Palacio Nacional

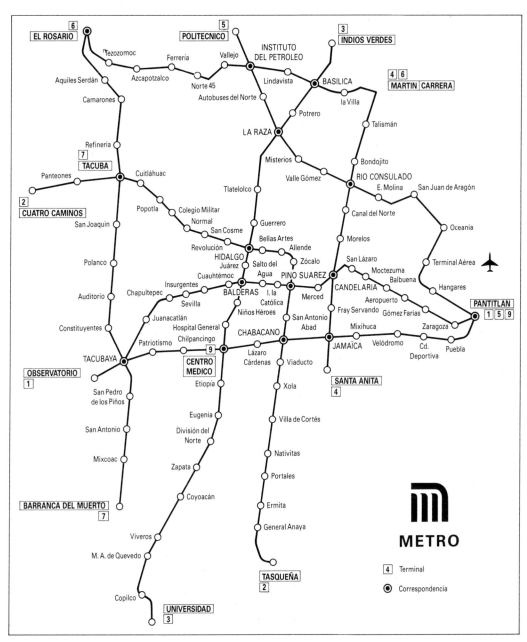

Mexico City's Metro system

taxis (radio-cabs) and the cheaper yellow taxis to be found in the street. These should charge according to the meter – *taxímetro* – but a combination of factors, both human and economic, conspire against this, so it is advisable to establish the fare beforehand. In view of the sheer size of the city, it is useful to have a fairly clear idea of where you are going, e.g.: *Insurgentes Sur entre Mixcoac y Barranca del Muerto; Revolución esquina con . . .* etc.

Mexican mural paintings

One of the major cultural attractions for visitors to Mexico City are the Rivera murals in the National Palace. The Muralist movement, which later inspired American artists such as Jackson Pollock, has its origins in the cultural renaissance which took place after the revolution of 1910. Encouraged by the government, artists covered the walls of public buildings with scenes depicting Mexico's past, man's struggle against injustice and oppression and the possibilities of future betterment.

The three major figures of the Muralist movement were Diego Rivera, David Alfaro Siqueiros and José Clemente Orozco (whose magnificent murals in the Hospicio Cabañas are a must for any visitor to Guadalajara). The styles of these painters are very different, as were their personalities. Rivera is the most internationally famous, not only for his prodigious output but also for his larger-than-life personality. The work of all three can be seen at the Palacio de Bellas Artes, alongside that of Rufino Tamayo, another of Mexico's great modern artists.

PRACTICAS

Can you . . .?

Complete the phrases in Spanish, starting with *¿me puede?*

a – help me with my luggage?
b – tell me what this street is called?
c – take me to the Museo de Antropología?
d – wait for me on the corner of Londres and (*con*) Florencia?
e – leave me opposite the cinema?
f – tell me where I can get a bus to la Alameda?

Crossed lines

These questions and answers have got mixed up. Sort them out.
1 ¿Queda muy lejos?
2 ¿Es usted de aquí?
3 ¿Cuánto cuesta?
4 ¿Y trae equipaje?
5 ¿Cuánto tiempo tarda?
6 ¿Cómo llego al aeropuerto?

a *Sí, dos maletas*
b *No, a tres cuadras*
c *Dos horas y media*
d *Sí, del D.F.*
e *En taxi o en metro*
f *Cincuenta mil pesos*

Over to you

You are looking for the Museo de Arte Moderno and you stop someone to ask the way. Say it in Spanish.

You:	Excuse me. How do I get to the Museum of Modern Art?
Transeúnte:	Pues depende. ¿Le gusta caminar? Si no, puede tomar un camión.
You:	Is it very far?
Transeúnte:	A unos quince minutos de aquí.
You:	That's fine. I can walk.
Transeúnte:	Entonces siga todo derechito hasta llegar al Museo.
You:	Is it on the right or the left?
Transeúnte:	A mano izquierda, antes de llegar a la entrada del Bosque de Chapultepec.
You:	Thank you very much.
Transeúnte:	De nada ¡Qué le vaya muy bien!

Lost!

These instructions have got jumbled up. Sort them out.

a da vuelta a saliendo y sigue el semáforo del hotel hasta la izquierda.
b ¿por cómo Avenida a la llego me favor decir Juárez puede?
c ¿de metro aquí hay estación por una?
d a hasta todo la Avenida Juárez siga llegar derecho

e   detrás la Alameda banco el está de
f   hay dos cuadras a a un sitio de de mano izquierda
    aquí taxis

Missing link

Fill in the gaps with the appropriate pronoun.

a   ¿Cuándo me llamas? **(Me/Te/Se)** – llamo en la
    tardecita.
b   A Alfonso y a mí **(nosotros/los/nos)** – gustan las
    películas mexicanas.
c   ¿Ves a Ana y a Patricia? **(Ellas/Los/Las)** – veo los
    fines de semana.
d   ¿A dónde tengo que llevar este paquete? Tiene que
    llevar – **(lo/te/se)** a Correos.
e   A mí no **(le/me/lo)** – gusta tomar el colectivo.
f   ¿Vas a comprar los boletos? Sí, **(los/me/ellos)** –
    voy a comprar hoy.
g   ¿Conoces a los padres de Jorge? Sí, **(nos/los/**
    ellos) – conozco muy bien.
h   Queremos comer. ¿**(Nos/nosotros/los)** – trae la
    carta, por favor?

Say it in Spanish

a   I can't see Juan today.
b   And what about you (*usted*) – do you like Mexico?
c   They can't take Angeles to the airport.
d   I like Mexican food. Do you (*tú*)?
e   We can wait for Susanita in the bar.
f   Mauricio likes big cities, but I don't.

Odd one out

a   allá, hola, allí, ahí
b   autobús, camión, automático, colectivo
c   glorieta, esquina, cuadra, maleta
d   parada, camión, sitio, estación
e   esperar, cobrar, pagar, costar
f   detrás, enfrente, delante, ahora
g   cruzar, ir a pie, ayudar, seguir

Sopa de Letras

Find in this rather peculiar type of soup the Spanish
words for **street**, **roundabout**, **block**, **avenue**,
district and **corner**. Be prepared to read backwards!

```
A  G  A  I  N  O  L  O  C
N  O  L  D  C  U  M  N  L
I  M  X  O  R  O  A  V  C
U  A  M  O  R  C  I  T  U
Q  L  A  E  O  I  N  P  A
S  A  C  A  L  L  E  R  D
E  M  O  M  A  T  A  T  R
R  V  A  D  I  N  E  V  A
```

¿Conoce usted México?

Say whether the statements are true or false.

a   El boleto es el baile típico de la Ciudad de México.
b   La Ciudad de México está en el norte del país.
c   México fue una colonia de España durante tres
    siglos.
d   El Templo Mayor es la iglesia principal de la ciudad
    de México.
e   El D.F. es un tipo de transporte colectivo.
f   México comparte fronteras con Belice, Venezuela y
    los Estados Unidos.
g   Tiene que comprar un boleto antes de tomar un taxi
    en el aeropuerto.
h   La Ciudad de México tiene quince millones de
    habitantes.

For the traveller to reflect on:
'Esperamos que de vuelta a sus lejanas tierras,
nuestros amigos lleven en sus pupilas, no sólo
la imagen del valle florido y limpio sino
también en sus corazones, el calor de nuestra
amistad.'

El Rey-poeta Nezahualcoyotl

2 México indígena

México, el último de los países mágicos; mágico de antigüedad y de historia, mágico de música y de geografía

Pablo Neruda

TRAVELLING AROUND MEXICO
CHECKING INTO A HOTEL
CHANGING MONEY

EN DIRECTO

1 Two young travellers go to a tourist office in Mexico City to find out about transport to Oaxaca.

Santiago:	Buenas noches, señorita.
Empleada:	Buenas noches. A sus órdenes.
Santiago:	Queremos saber cómo podemos ir a Oaxaca.
Empleada:	Se puede ir en avión o en autobús. En avión es muy rápido – el vuelo dura cincuenta minutos. El autobús tarda ocho horas pero es mucho más barato. Cuesta treinta y cinco mil pesos, ida y vuelta, en primera.
Patricia:	¿Y tiene aire acondicionado y baño?
Empleada:	Sí, claro.
Patricia:	¿Aquí se venden los boletos?
Empleada:	No. Tienen que ir directamente a la central de autobuses al lado del metro San Lázaro. Miren, aquí tienen un plano. (*She hands them a map.*)
Santiago:	Muy bien. Muchas gracias.
Empleada:	De nada. ¡Qué les vaya bien!

saber	*to know*
autobús	*coach* (Mex)
baño	*toilet* (Mex)
central de autobuses (Mex)	*bus station*

● **Spot-check 1**
1 How much longer does the bus take than the plane?
2 Do Santiago and Patricia buy their tickets at the tourist office?

> To say something has to be done, use **tener que** + infinitive:
> **tienen que ir** you have to go
> **tengo que trabajar** I have to work

> To say how long something lasts:
> el vuelo **dura** 50 minutos
> la película **dura** casi 2 horas

> To say how long something takes:
> el autobus **tarda** 8 horas
> el avión **tarda** menos que el tren

2 The next morning Santiago and Patricia go to the coach station.

Patricia:	Buenos días.
Dependiente:	Buenos días.
Patricia:	Quiero dos boletos de ida y vuelta para Oaxaca, por favor.
Dependiente:	¿A qué hora desea salir?
Patricia:	En la próxima salida.
Dependiente:	A las nueve entonces. ¿Qué lugar prefiere?
Patricia:	En medio, por favor.
Dependiente:	Ya no quedan dos asientos juntos. (*Pointing to seating plan*) Tengo un asiento de ventanilla aquí, y otro asiento acá, en el pasillo.
Patricia:	Está bien.
Dependiente:	Son setenta mil pesos.
Patricia:	Aquí tiene. (*She pays.*) ¿Por qué puerta sale?
Dependiente:	Por la puerta cuarenta y seis.
Patricia:	Gracias.

lugar	place
en medio	in the middle
Ya no quedan dos asientos	There aren't two seats
juntos	together
de ventanilla	window
pasillo	aisle
puerta	gate

● **Spot-check 2**

1 Do Santiago and Patricia manage to get two seats together in the middle?
2 From which gate does the coach leave?

Time-telling

The 24-hour clock is used in Mexico, as elsewhere, for times of planes, trains etc. But in informal speech, there are a few expressions peculiar to Mexico. *Para la(s)* is used instead of *menos* to mean 'to':

cuarto para las cinco	quarter to five
(faltan) cinco para las tres	five to three

Con can be used as well as *y* to mean 'past':

las tres con veinticinco   twenty-five past three
  (minutos)

And to ask what the time is: *¿qué horas son?*

¡Ya!

This little word has various meanings depending on
the context. When used with the negative it means
'no longer':

ya no hay asientos en la sección de no fumar
ya no quedan boletos para mañana

3 In Oaxaca, Yolanda García checks into the Hotel
Presidente, a converted seventeenth-century convent
and one of the sights of the city.

Yolanda:	Buenas tardes.
Recepcionista:	Buenas tardes, señora.
Yolanda:	Tengo una reservación a nombre de Yolanda García Caballero.
Recepcionista:	(*Looking at list*) Señora García . . . ah, sí. Es por tres noches. (*He hands over the registration form and points to it.*) ¿Quiere poner su nombre y su dirección aquí? ¿Cómo va a pagar – en efectivo o con tarjeta de crédito?
Yolanda:	Con tarjeta de crédito.
Recepcionista:	¿Me permite su tarjeta, por favor?
Yolanda:	Sí, cómo no. (*She hands over the card.*)
Recepcionista:	Gracias. (*He stamps the form.*) ¿Puede firmar? (*Yolanda signs.*) Gracias. Su habitación es la ciento veintitrés. Ahorita le suben su equipaje.
Yolanda:	Muchas gracias.
Recepcionista:	Para servirle.

reservación (Mex)	*reservation*
a nombre de	*in the name of*
dirección	*address*
en efectivo	*in cash*
¿me permite?	*may I see...?*
cómo no	*of course*
ahorita (Mex)	*in a few minutes*

● **Spot-check 3** 1 How long is Yolanda staying?
2 Does she pay with cash?

Ahorita

In Spanish, adding *-ito/-ita/-itos/-itas* to the end of a
word adds the meaning 'little':

una casa	a house
una casita	a little house
un pueblo	a village
un pueblito	a small village

These diminutive endings, as they are called, can
also add a sense of endearment:

mi abuelita	my granny
mi hermanito	my little brother

In Mexico, the diminutive form is used more widely than in Spain, though the original sense of 'little' is often absent. You may be offered *una sopita* or *un cafecito* in a restaurant; you might hear the direction *derechito*.

You will often be asked to wait *un momentito* in an office or on the phone. A friend will tell you that he/she is going to arrive *un poquito tarde*, which doesn't mean in ten minutes. In the classic *ahorita*, the diminutive ending has the effect of diminishing the immediacy of *ahora*: it can mean anything from half an hour to infinity. To be unpunctual in Mexico is not considered impolite; to say bluntly 'no/never/impossible' is a mark of discourtesy.

4 Beatriz Fregoso goes to *una casa de cambio* to change some travellers' cheques.

Beatriz:	Buenos días.
Empleado:	Buenos días.
Beatriz:	Quiero cambiar unos cheques de viajero. ¿A cómo está el dólar?
Empleado:	A dos mil quinientos treinta pesos.
Beatriz:	Entonces voy a cambiar cien dólares.
Empleado:	¿Tiene usted alguna identificación?
Beatriz:	Sí, tengo mi pasaporte. (*She hands over the passport and points to the cheques.*) ¿Firmo?

unos cheques de viajero	*some travellers' cheques*
¿a cómo está el dólar?	*What's the (exchange) rate for the dollar?*
alguna	*any*

Empleado:	Sí, por favor.
Beatriz:	¿Qué día es hoy?
Empleado:	Es el dos de mayo. (*Beatriz hands over the cheques: she is given a receipt.*) Pase a la siguiente ventanilla, por favor.
Beatriz:	Gracias. (*Beatriz waits for the number on her receipt to be called out.*)
Cajera:	Número doscientos quince. ¿Me da su forma, por favor? (*Beatriz hands over the receipt.*) Son doscientos cincuenta y tres mil pesos. (*Counting out the money*) . . . Cincuenta . . . cien . . . ciento cincuenta . . . doscientos . . . doscientos cincuenta mil . . . uno, dos, tres mil.
Beatriz:	Gracias. Hasta luego.
Cajera:	Hasta luego.

pase a   *go to*
siguiente   *next*

forma   *form*

● **Spot-check 4**

1 What's the exchange rate for the dollar?
2 Why does she show her passport?

To ask the date:
¿qué día es hoy?
To say what the date is:
es el dos de mayo

Pase usted

There are two main uses for the verb *pasar*:

1 movement

pase a la caja	go to the till
pase usted	please go/come in
¿se puede pasar?	can I come in?
van a pasar por mí a las dos	they're going to pick me up at two.

2 time

voy a pasar un mes en Mérida	I'm going to spend a month in Mérida
¡qué lo pases bien!	have a good time!

VOCABULARIO

el asiento	*seat*
el autobús	*coach* (Mex)
el baño	*toilet* (Mex)
la central camionera/de autobuses (Mex)	*coach station*

la caja	till/cash desk
el lugar	place
el pasillo	aisle
la ventanilla	window (in a car/plane etc.)
la casa de cambio	bureau de change
la forma	form (Mex)
la fecha	date
el billete	bank note
el nombre	name
el apellido	surname
la dirección	address
la reservación (Mex)	reservation
la caja de seguridad	safe deposit box
la alberca	swimming pool (Mex)
el elevador (Mex)	lift
la regadera	shower (Mex)
durar	to last
tardar	to take (a length of time)
quedar	to remain/be left
reservar	to reserve
pasar	to go to/to pass by
levantarse	to get up
acostarse	to go to bed
en efectivo	in cash
en medio	in the middle
junto	together
separado	separate
siguiente	next
ya no	no longer

ASI SE DICE

To say something has to be done, use
tener que + infinitive:

tienen que ir	you have to go
tengo que trabajar	I have to work

To ask the date:
¿qué día es hoy?
To say what the date is:
es el dos de mayo

To talk about when things usually happen:

los martes	on Tuesdays
todos los martes	every Tuesday
los fines de semana	at weekends
todos los fines de semana	every weekend
entre semana	on weekdays

To say how long something lasts:
el vuelo **dura** 3 horas
To say how long something takes:
el autobús **tarda** 8 horas
¿vas a **tardar** mucho?
To say how long it takes to do something, use
tardar en + infinitive:
¿cuánto tiempo **tardas en** llegar?
tardo 10 minutos **en llegar** a la oficina
In Mexico, tardar is often used reflexively:

no me tardo nada	I won't be long

NOTAS DE LENGUA

Asking politely

There are various polite ways of asking someone to do something. In dialogue 3, the hotel receptionist asks:

¿quiere poner...?	would you like to put...?
¿puede firmar?	could you sign?

In dialogue 4, the cashier puts the instruction in the form of a question:

¿me da su forma?	would you give me your form?

Notice that the Spanish is more direct than the English, though equally polite. ¿Quiere? – literally 'do you want . . .?' – can be used to mean 'would you like . . .?'; ¿puede . . .? – literally 'can you . . .?' – can be used to mean 'could you . . .?'

On written instructions you may see:
favor de/se ruega no dejar maletas en el pasillo
please do not leave luggage in the corridor

Imperative needs

The most direct way of giving instructions is to use what is known as the 'imperative' form of the verb:

pase a la siguiente ventanilla	go to the next window
repita la frase	repeat the sentence
lea las instrucciones	read the instructions
dejen de fumar	refrain from smoking

You will often hear the imperative used in directions:
siga *por esta calle*
tome *la primera a la izquierda*
In Mexico you will see *jale* (pull) and *empuje* (push) on doors.

When talking to someone you would address as *usted*, the imperative is formed by taking the first person singular of the verb, removing the *-o* ending and replacing it as follows:

-e in the case of *-ar* verbs: *hable, tome*
-a in the case of *-er* and *-ir* verbs: *viva, suba*

This rule usually applies to irregular verbs:
tenga, diga, ponga
But there are exceptions:
vaya (ir), dé (dar)
For the *ustedes* form of the imperative, simply add *-n* to the *usted* form:
hablen, tomen, sigan

Reflect on this

Compare the two sentences:
Peter wakes up John
Peter wakes up
In the first sentence Peter is waking someone else, in the second sentence he is waking himself. In Spanish these sentences become:
Pedro despierta a Juan
Pedro se despierta
The *se* makes it clear that Pedro is waking himself and is known as a reflexive pronoun. The complete list of reflexive pronouns is:
yo **me** *despierto*
tú **te** *despiertas*
usted/él/ella **se** *despierta*
nosotros **nos** *despertamos*
vosotros **os** *despertáis*
ustedes/ellos/ellas **se** *despiertan*

Don't forget that the *vosotros* form is not used in Mexico.

When the verb is in the infinitive, the reflexive pronoun usually joins on to it:
quiero bañarme
tenemos que levantarnos temprano

In the imperative, the pronoun joins on to the end of the verb:

¡siéntense!	sit down
¡abróchense los cinturones de seguridad!	fasten your seat belts

But if it is a negative command, the pronoun precedes the verb:

¡no se preocupe!	don't worry
¡no se moleste!	don't go to any trouble

In Mexico, you will hear the reflexive pronoun used more widely than in Spain.

LECTURAS

Los tapetes de Teotitlán

Para los indígenas de Oaxaca, la artesanía ha sido tradicionalmente una forma de complementar unos ingresos muy escasos: el estado es uno de los más pobres de México.

En los últimos tiempos, sin embargo, se ha producido una revalorización de la producción artesanal: debido a la presión del mercado, algunos artesanos han adoptado técnicas más modernas e industriales, abandonando las más tradicionales.

Pero artesanos como los Mendoza, indios zapotecas, han conservado los métodos de sus antepasados. Se dedican a la fabricación de tapetes, un negocio floreciente en el pueblo de Teotitlán.

En casa de los Mendoza, toda la lana se hila y tiñe a mano. Para el teñido, se utilizan productos naturales de la comarca, como el musgo de roca o la cochinilla. En el diseño de los tapetes, se usan motivos zapotecas, anteriores a la conquista de los españoles. Aunque Emiliano, el padre, también ha realizado encargos de arte abstracto, dice preferir los diseños más antiguos: 'Es una tradición de nuestra raza zapoteca. . . Y es eso, que a mí me encanta también no perder lo tradicional'.

El caso de los Mendoza es un buen ejemplo de como la vida moderna, en algunos aspectos, puede contribuir a mantener viva la identidad de los grupos indígenas.

Abigail Mendoza at work

1   Why do the Indians of Oaxaca have to supplement their income?
2   Why have some artisans abandoned the traditional methods?
3   What two types of design do the Mendoza family make?

Médicos y curanderos

En muchas de las comunidades de Oaxaca, como en el pueblo de Tlaxiaco, la medicina indígena todavía sigue viva.

Los puestos de plantas medicinales, que venden remedios para casi todos los males, son típicos de cualquier mercado. Y los tradicionales médicos indígenas, los curanderos, siguen practicando sus artes de curación.

Angélica Hernández ha sido curandera en Tlaxiaco desde que era muy joven. Además de utilizar plantas, Angélica reconoce la importancia de la religión católica en el proceso de curación: 'el factor más importante es la fe'.

La medicina moderna, sin embargo, también está presente en el pueblo. Hay un hospital del estado, y el doctor Javier Bautista da clases de educación sanitaria en las escuelas. Javier piensa que, 'El médico moderno se olvida de muchas cosas que el médico indígena sí alcanza a ver, como es la familia, el medio en que vive esta gente'.

El doctor cree que un equilibrio entre la medicina moderna e indígena es necesario para asegurar el bienestar y el futuro de los indígenas mexicanos.

1   What is a *curandero*?
2   Does Angélica rely solely on herbal medicines in the healing process?
3   What does Dr. Bautista think is wrong with modern medicine?

EXTRA

A Señor and Señora Arizmendi arrive late at their hotel.

Turista:	Buenas noches. Tenemos una reservación a nombre de Arizmendi.
Recepcionista:	Buenas noches. Bienvenidos . . . ah, acaban de llegar del aerópuerto, ¿no?
Turista:	Sí. Tuvimos que esperar una hora y media en Tampico.
Recepcionista:	¡Ay, qué pesado! Nada más les voy a molestar con esta forma. ¿Van a pagar con tarjeta de crédito?
Turista:	Sí, aquí tiene.
Recepcionista:	Gracias.
Turista:	El restaurante está cerrado, ¿no?
Recepcionista:	Sí, cierra a las 11, pero hay servicio a cuartos. En su habitación van a encontrar el menú. Para ordenar hay que marcar el 04.
Turista:	Mañana tenemos que levantarnos temprano, ¿podría llamarnos a las seis y media, por favor?
Recepcionista:	¡Cómo no! Pueden desayunar en su habitacíon, si quieren.
Turista:	Muy amable. Muchas gracias.
Recepcionista:	Para servirles. ¡Qué descansen! Hasta mañana.

bienvenidos *welcome*
acaban de llegar *you've just arrived*
tuvimos que... *we had to...*
¡Ay, qué pesado! *what a nuisance!*
Nada más les voy a molestar... *could I just trouble you...?*
servicio a cuartos *room service*
ordenar (Mex) *order*
hay que marcar *you have to dial*
temprano *early*
¿podría...? *could you...?*
¡Qué descansen! *Have a good rest/sleep well!*

¿Verdad? Are these statements true or false?
1 Los Arizmendi quieren levantarse temprano.
2 Los Arizmendi van a cenar en el restaurante.

B A passenger is checking in at the airport.

Pasajera:	¿Es aquí donde se documenta para el vuelo a Veracruz?
Empleado:	Sí, señorita. ¿Me permite su boleto? ¿Viaja sola?
Pasajera:	Sí.
Empleado:	Pues, mejor sola que mal acompañada, ¿no? El vuelo a Veracruz tiene un pequeño retraso. Después de documentar su equipaje, le recomiendo que tome un cafecito mientras espera la salida de su vuelo.
Pasajera:	¿Va a demorarse mucho?
Empleado:	Una hora más o menos. Salió tarde del puerto por el mal tiempo en el Golfo.
Pasajera:	¡Vaya!
Empleado:	Tranquilícese. No tiene importancia. A ver . . . una maleta, ¿no? ¿Y trae equipaje de mano?
Pasajera:	Sí, esta bolsa.
Empleado:	¿Qué quiere, ventanilla o pasillo?
Pasajera:	Pasillo – y no fumar.

pasajera *passenger*
se documenta (Mex) *check in*
retraso *delay*
mientras *while*
demorarse *to be delayed*
salió tarde *it left late*
¡vaya! *oh dear!*
tranquilícese *don't worry*
bolsa *bag*

Empleado:	Muy bien. Aquí tiene su tarjeta de abordar. En cuanto anuncien el vuelo pase a la Sala B, por favor.	**tarjeta de abordar** (Mex)	*boarding card*
Pasajera:	Gracias.	**en cuanto**	*as soon as*
Empleado:	Para servirle.	**sala**	*departure lounge*

¿Verdad? 1 El empleado quiere tomar un cafecito con la pasajera.

2 La pasajera quiere fumar en el avión.

C A visitor wants to fly to Huatulco, a new tourist centre on the Pacific coast.

Turista:	¿Tiene usted alguna información sobre los vuelos a Huatulco?		
Empleada:	Claro que sí. Hay un vuelo diario que sale a las doce cincuenta y cinco, y hace escala en Oaxaca; llega a Huatulco a las catorce cincuenta.	**diario** **hace escala**	*daily* *stops over*
Turista:	¿Y no hay otro vuelo?		
Empleada:	No. Es el único.		
Turista:	Entonces, ¿podría hacerme la reservación para este sábado?		
Empleada:	Lo siento, este fin de semana los vuelos están llenos.		
Turista:	Entonces, para el próximo lunes.		
Empleada:	¿Ida y vuelta?		
Turista:	No sé cuando voy a regresar. Quiero un boleto abierto.	**no sé**	*I don't know*
Empleada:	Déjeme checar si hay lugar . . . Sí, no hay problema. ¿A qué nombre?	**checar** (Mex)	*check*
Turista:	Juventino Sánchez.		
Empleada:	Muy bien, señor Sánchez. Usted tiene la reservación para el lunes 14 en el vuelo de Mexicana.		

¿Verdad? 1 El vuelo a Huatulco es directo.

2 Juventino no quiere un boleto de ida y vuelta.

D A guest in a hotel has a noisy room which she wants to change.

Turista:	Buenos días.		
Recepcionista:	Hola, buenos días ¿cómo le va?	**¿cómo le va?**	*how are you?*
Turista:	Pues, francamente no muy bien. Mi habitación da a la calle y no puedo dormir. Hoy me desperté a las 6, con el ruido del tráfico. ¿No podría cambiar de habitación?	**francamente** **da a** **me desperté** **ruido**	*frankly* *looks onto* *I woke up* *noise*
Recepcionista:	Vamos a ver: sí, tenemos la 415 – está en el cuarto piso, en la parte de atrás, así que es muy tranquila. El único problema es que no tiene terraza.	**de atrás** **terraza** **así que**	*rear* *balcony* *so that*

Turista:	No me importa. Prefiero la tranquilidad.		
Recepcionista:	Muy bien. Al ratito le ayudamos con sus cosas.	**al ratito**	*in a moment*
Turista:	Gracias.	**sus cosas**	*your things*

¿Verdad? 1 El turista quiere cambiar de habitación porque no puede dormir.

2 La habitación 415 tiene terraza.

A *conchero* dancer performing in a festival for the Virgin of Guadalupe

MEXICO VIVO

Mexican Indians

The Indian groups in Mexico – *los grupos indígenas* – make up almost a fifth of the country's population according to one estimate from the Instituto Nacional Indigenista. Of the 150 or so groups that existed before the Conquest, over 50 still survive with their own language and cultures. The two largest are the Nahuas of Central Mexico and the Mayas from the south-east.

70% of Indians speak some Spanish even if it is not their first language. Nearly all of them are Roman Catholic, though in their religious practices they combine elements of pre-Hispanic ritual. One example of this is the cult of the dead, celebrated on November 1 and 2, *el Día de los Muertos*, when the souls of the dead are believed to return to earth. Food is prepared for dead relatives, altars are decorated with flowers and skulls and an all-night vigil is kept in the cemeteries. Children give each other sugar skulls – *calaveras.*

Despite Mexico's pride in its Indian roots, indigenous communities are still the most deprived section of the population. The dilemma today is how to bring them the benefits of modern life without also destroying their culture and their identity.

Crafts

The wonderful variety of Mexican crafts reflects the diversity of the Indian groups. Originally produced to satisfy the practical needs of the Indians themselves, their crafts now provide a valuable source of income. Some go back to pre-Hispanic days, others were introduced by the Spaniards, who trained the Indians to use new materials and techniques.

The central and southern areas of Mexico are particularly rich in crafts. Most state capitals have *una Casa de Artesanías* offering the specialities of the area; Indian markets are another source. Some of the most popular buys for visitors are:

amate	painted tree bark
cerámica	all types of ceramic-ware, from pots and plates to elaborately sculpted trees of life
laca	lacquered wood
orfebrería	metal-work, especially gold and silver, often based on pre-Hispanic designs
tapetes	rugs
huipiles	embroidered smocks
sarapes	blankets
rebozos	shawls
camisas bordadas	embroidered shirts
guayaberas	short-sleeved shirts
máscaras	masks, including wooden ones in the shape of jaguars, devils and old men

Oaxaca

Oaxaca is a mountainous state 300 miles south of Mexico City. It has one of the largest Indian populations of any Mexican state and the greatest number of different indigenous groups. The first Indian president of Mexico, Benito Juárez, came from Oaxaca: he was a pure-blooded Zapotec who became one of Mexico's most revered presidents in 1858. The capital of the state is named in his honour Oaxaca de Juárez.

The capital is a charming city in a lovely hilly setting. It encapsulates Mexico's past and present. It has fine

colonial buildings and colourful Indian markets –
including the famous Saturday market, reputed to be
the biggest in Mexico. Oaxaca is also a good base for
visiting some magnificent archaeological sites,
former ceremonial centres of the Zapotec and Mixtec
cultures which flourished long before the Spanish
conquest.

One of the many attractions of Oaxaca for visitors is
the variety of its crafts – particularly its textiles and
metalwork. As well as carpets and rugs, many types
of richly-coloured clothing are produced – cotton
blouses and skirts, belts and sashes, *sarapes* and
rebozos. A gold-mining centre under the Spanish,
Oaxaca still specialises in exquisite gold jewellery
based on that found at the nearby Mixtec site of
Monte Albán; silver-ware and *hojalatería* – decorative
tin-ware – are also popular. In addition, there are
painted wooden animals and masks and a wide
range of ceramics, including the famous black
pottery.

Long-distance buses

The most economical way of travelling around the
country is by long-distance bus – *camión* or *autobús*.
They are operated by a vast number of companies.

Primera clase means a faster, more comfortable
service, with air-conditioning and a toilet. *Segunda
clase* can be a fascinating experience for short
journeys. At holiday times it is essential to book
tickets in advance. It is advisable to take a sweater/
jacket for travelling as the air-conditioning can be
glacially efficient: this problem doesn't arise in
segunda clase – the chickens keep you warm.

Trains (*Ferrocarriles Nacionales de México*)

Recently the Government has embarked on a
programme to revitalise the passenger rail network
and in the face of higher air-fares trains are proving a
popular and acceptable alternative. It is an excellent
way of seeing the countryside at a leisurely pace. The
most spectacular scenery is on the *Chihuahua-
Pacífico* route through the majestic Copper Canyon,
la Barranca del Cobre.

It is important to make reservations in advance. On
overnight journeys there is a range of sleeping
accommodation available.

Take note!

Banks are open on weekdays from 9 am–1.30 pm.
Casas de cambio – bureaux de change – stay open
longer, until late afternoon.

You can change money in hotels but they may charge
above the official rate (*tipo de cambio*). It is advisable
to take travellers' cheques in dollars, rather than
pounds sterling.

With inflation, smaller denominations of currency are
disappearing. There are coins of 10, 20, 50, 100,
200, 500 and 1,000 pesos, and notes of 2,000,
5,000, 10,000, 20,000 and 50,000 pesos. It is
common for Mexicans to say *doscientos* (for
200,000), *quinientos* (500,000) etc. so do be aware
of this phenomenon!

In colloquial language, *plata* (silver) is used to mean
dinero, as is *billete*. *Un platal* or *un dineral* means a
lot of money. *Lana* (wool) in slang means money and
younger Mexicans will say *me costó dos melones*
(millions).

PRACTICAS

Say it in Spanish

a I have to change some travellers' cheques.
b How long does the flight to Villahermosa take?
c Santiago and Patricia have to go to the bus terminal.
d What's the exchange rate for the dollar?
e What's today's date?
f Can I pay with a credit card?
g Juan cannot work on Saturdays.
h What do you (*tú*) do at weekends?

The other half

Match the following:

1 una central   a de crédito
2 un boleto   b con aire acondicionado

3 un plano   c   de cincuenta mil pesos
4 una tarjeta   d   de avíon
5 un billete   e   del centro histórico
6 un autobús   f   camionera

Over to you

You are in the airline office trying to get a ticket. Say it in Spanish.

Empleado:	Buenas tardes, señorita. A sus órdenes.
You:	*Good afternoon. I want to go to Acapulco tomorrow morning if possible.*
Empleado:	Lo siento, pero no hay lugar. Tiene que esperar al miércoles.
You:	*All right. What time is the flight?*
Empleado:	Hay dos vuelos. Uno sale a las 8 de la mañana, el otro a las 4 de la tarde.
You:	*I prefer the morning flight.*
Empleado:	Muy bien. ¿Me da su nombre y su teléfono, por favor?
You:	*Of course . . . and here is my credit card.*

Answer back

Match the questions and answers.

1 ¿Se puede fumar?
2 ¿Se puede cambiar cheques de viajero?
3 ¿Se puede comer en el hotel?
4 ¿Se puede depositar dinero y valores?
5 ¿Se puede nadar?
6 ¿Se puede pagar con tarjeta de crédito?

a *No, no tenemos alberca.*
b *No, está prohibido.*
c *Sí, en la caja de seguridad.*
d *No, pero hay un restaurante a dos cuadras.*
e *Sí, en la caja de enfrente.*
f *No, sólo en efectivo.*

Order please

Give the following instructions in Spanish using the *usted* form.

a Call the taxi-rank, please!
b Close the door, please!
c Sign here, please!
d Wait a moment, please!
e Leave me on the corner, please!

Now ask if people can do these things using the verb *poder.*

Missing link

Fill in the gaps with the appropriate reflexive pronoun.

a —llaman Pedro y Cristina.
b ¿—diviertes aquí?
c ¡No—preocupe!
d Vamos a levantar—a las seis.
e ¡Siénten—, por favor!
f —baño cada día en la alberca.
g ¡Súba—por la puerta de delante!

In the right order

You arrive at the hotel in a taxi. In which sequence would you do the following?

a Desempacar la maleta
b Salir a dar un paseo
c Bajarse en el elevador
d Registrarse en la recepción
e Pagar al taxista
f Subirse a la habitación

Over to you

Play the role of the tourist at the bus-station.

Empleado:	Buenas tardes.
You:	*Good afternoon. I want two tickets to Mexico City.*
Empleado:	¿Para cuándo?
You:	*For the departure at 1 1 pm tonight.*
Empleado:	¿Qué lugar prefiere?
You:	*Are there two seats in the middle?*
Empleado:	Ya no quedan dos asientos juntos. Pero sí hay dos atrás.
You:	*Are there any at the front?*
Empleado:	Quedan dos lugares – pero no están juntos.
You:	*We prefer to be together. Give us the two at the back, please.*
Empleado:	Está bien. Son sesenta y ocho mil pesos.

A question of time

Fill in the gaps with the appropriate form of *tardar* or *durar*.

a El viaje al pueblo de Teotitlán—una media hora.
b ¿Y cuántos meses—la época de lluvias?
c Donaciano va a—unos diez minutos en llegar aquí.
d Este año, la primavera—en llegar.
e Para ir al trabajo, yo—una media hora.

Excuses, excuses

Say it in Spanish.

a I can't help. I have to go to the airport.
b You (*tú*) can't go. You have to work tonight.
c We can't wait. We have to take a flight to Acapulco.
d They can't come. They have to see a friend tonight.
e She can't talk now. You have to come tomorrow.

Hotel rules

Read the following extracts from the *directorio de servicios* of a Mexican hotel, then answer the questions in English.

RECEPCION:
Aquí puede usted solicitar todos estos servicios: cambio de moneda (no se aceptan cheques personales); cajas de seguridad; información; servicio médico; despertador.

PROPINAS
Se sugiere un 15% en todos los servicios.

HORARIO DE SALIDA
Los huéspedes deben checar la salida antes de las 12 horas.

ALBERCA
Se puede utilizar de 7 am a 8 pm. Se ruega a los huéspedes usar la regadera antes de bañarse.

a Can you change money at the reception desk?
b Where do you go to ask for a safe deposit box?
c What is the recommended tip?
d What are guests asked to do before using the swimming pool?
e What is the latest check-out time?
f Can you pay with a personal cheque?

Crucigrama

Fill in the horizontal words and a secret word will appear in the shaded vertical line.

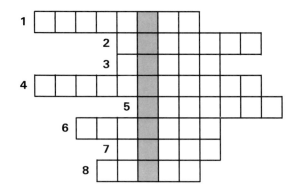

1 shower
2 swimming pool
3 date
4 booking
5 seat
6 to take time
7 form
8 to last

¿Conoce usted México?

Are the following statements true or false?

a Los grupos indígenas son bandas de música local.
b Las casas de cambio tienen un horario más largo que los bancos.
c Los zapotecas son un tipo especial de zapatos.
d Benito Juárez es el presidente actual de México.
e Oaxaca es famoso por su artesanía.
f Los sarapes y la orfebrería son formas de artesanía.
g Se hablan más de cincuenta lenguas indígenas en México.
h Los tapetes se sirven como aperitivo antes de comer.

3 Somos gente de maíz

> Maíz, sociedad, cultura e historia son inseparables. Nuestro pasado y nuestro presente tienen su fundamento en el maíz . . . somos gente de maíz.
>
> Guillermo Bonfil Batalla

The Aztec Maize God and Goddess, Centéotl and Centeocíhuatl

MAKING ARRANGEMENTS TO MEET
MAKING A TELEPHONE CALL
ORDERING BREAKFAST

EN DIRECTO

1 Verónica Cruz phones a friend to arrange to meet for lunch at *una taquería* – a restaurant specialising in *tacos*, stuffed maize pancakes.

Rosa:	¡Bueno!
Verónica:	Rosa, habla Verónica. ¿Cómo has estado?
Rosa:	¡Verónica! Muy bien gracias. ¡Qué gusto oirte! ¿Estás aquí en México?
Verónica:	Sí, acabo de llegar. Tengo muchas ganas de platicar contigo.
Rosa:	Sí, yo también.
Verónica:	¿Cuándo nos vemos?
Rosa:	Pues, hoy en la tarde, si quieres.
Verónica:	¡Ay, qué pena! Hoy no puedo. Tengo un compromiso. Pero mañana estoy libre. ¿Por qué no nos vemos para comer unos tacos en la Casa Beatriz?
Rosa:	Sí, perfecto. ¿A qué hora?
Verónica:	¿A las dos te parece bien?
Rosa:	Sí, sí.
Verónica:	Puedo pasar por ti si quieres.
Rosa:	Muy bien. Hasta mañana entonces.

¿Cómo has estado?	*How have you been?*
¡Qué gusto oirte!	*it's good to hear you*
tengo . . . ganas de	*I want to . . .*
platicar	*to chat (Mex)*
también	*too*
¡qué pena!	*what a shame!*
compromiso	*engagement*
libre	*free*

Verónica:	Te mando un abrazo.	**te mando**	*(literally) I send*
Rosa:	Yo también.		*you*
Verónica:	Hasta luego.	**abrazo**	*hug*

● **Spot-check 1**   1 When does Verónica have an engagement?
2 At what time are the friends going to meet?

> *To say 'hello' when answering the phone:*
> **¡bueno!** (Mex)
> *To say who's speaking:*
> **habla Verónica**

> *To say you've just done something:*
> **acabo de** | **llegar**
> | **ver a Rosa**

> *To suggest an arrangement:*
> **¿por qué no** | **nos vemos mañana?**
> | **vamos al cine?**
> *To ask if an arrangement is acceptable:*
> **¿te/le/les parece bien?**

¿Te parece bien?

Parecer means 'to seem' or 'to appear':
parece que sí it seems so
The reflexive form *parecerse* means literally 'to look like':
te pareces mucho a tu hermana
The phrase *¿qué te parece?* is used when asking someone how they feel about something. One way of replying would be:
me parece muy bien/mal
¿te parece? on its own means 'OK?/Is that all right?'.

En la tarde

Whereas in Spain, 'in the morning/afternoon' etc. is *por la mañana, por la tarde*, in Mexico you will hear *en la mañana, en la tarde*.

2   In the Executive Suite of a Mexico City hotel, Yolanda Hinojosa asks if she can use the phone.

Yolanda:	Buenos días, señorita.		
Recepcionista:	Buenos días.		
Yolanda:	¿Podría utilizar su teléfono, por favor?	**utilizar**	*use*

Recepcionista:	¡Cómo no! Hay uno aquí al lado. Hay que marcar el cero, esperar el tono y despúes marcar el número.	**hay que marcar**	*you have to dial*
Yolanda:	Muchas gracias.		
Recepcionista:	De nada.		
	(*Yolanda dials the number.*)		
Secretaria:	¡Bueno!		
Yolanda:	Buenos días, señorita. ¿Podría hablar con el licenciado Mendoza, por favor?		
Secretaria:	Lo siento, pero no se encuentra en este momento. ¿Quiere dejar un recado?	**no se encuentra**	*he's not here*
Yolanda:	Sí, por favor.	**recado**	*message*
Secretaria:	¿De parte de quién?		
Yolanda:	De la licenciada Hinojosa.		
Secretaria:	¿Cómo se escribe?		
Yolanda:	Hinojosa – H I N O J O S A. ¿Podría preguntarle si es posible adelantar la cita de mañana, y vernos a las ocho en el Sanborns de Madero para desayunar?	**adelantar** **cita** **el Sanborns de Madero**	*bring forward* *appointment* *Sanborns restaurant in la calle de Madero*
Secretaria:	Sí, con mucho gusto. Yo le paso su recado.		
Yolanda:	Muy amable. Hasta luego.		
Secretaria:	Hasta luego.		

● **Spot-check 2**

1 Which number does Yolanda have to dial to get a line?
2 Why can't Lic. Mendoza speak on the phone?

To ask if something would be possible:
¿podría | **utilizar su teléfono?**
hablar con el director?
preguntarle si puede venir?
*Note that **¿podría . . .?** means 'could I . . .?' and 'could you/she/he . . .?'*

To ask who's speaking:
¿de parte de quién?

To ask how something is spelt:
¿cómo se escribe?
For the pronunciation of letters in Spanish see page 96

It's a must
In chapter 2 we saw that *tener que* + infinitive is used to say what someone has to do:
tengo que llamarle

tienes que comer más
A more impersonal way of saying what has to be done is to use *hay que* + infinitive:
hay que marcar el O
hay que presentarse en el aeropuerto una hora antes del vuelo

3 Yolanda arrives late for her meeting with Sergio Mendoza.

Yolanda:	Hola.
Sergio:	Buenos días.
Yolanda:	Buenos días. ¡Perdóneme! Siento llegar tan tarde, pero el tránsito estaba muy pesado hoy.
Mesera:	Buenos días. ¿Les tomo su orden?
Yolanda:	Buenos días. Yo quiero un jugo de toronja, un plato de frutas frescas y hot cakes con miel.
Sergio:	Y para mí, un jugo de piña, unos huevos revueltos y pan tostado, por favor.
Mesera:	Muy bien.

tránsito	*traffic*
estaba	*was*
pesado	*bad*
mesera (Mex)	*waitress*
orden (Mex)	*order*
jugo de toronja (Mex)	*grapefruit juice*
hot cakes con miel (Mex)	*Scotch pancakes with syrup*
piña	*pineapple*
huevos revueltos	*scrambled eggs*

● **Spot-check 3** 1 Why does Yolanda arrive late?
2 Do they both order fruit juices?

> *To apologise for something:*
> **siento** | **llegar tarde**
> | **molestarle**

VOCABULARIO

la llamada	*phone call*
la oficina	*office*
el compromiso	*prior engagement*
la cita	*appointment*
el recado	*message*
el abrazo	*hug*
libre	*free*
ocupado	*busy*
tan	*so*
temprano	*early*
tarde	*late*
llamar	*to call/to phone*
confirmar	*to confirm*
cancelar	*to cancel*
marcar	*to dial*

Sanborns in la Calle de Madero, Mexico City

platicar	to chat (Mex)
encontrarse	to be in a place
utilizar	to use
repetir	to repeat
volver	to return
volver a + infinitive	to do again
parecer	to seem/to appear
tener hambre	to be hungry
tener sed	to be thirsty
hay que + infinitive	it is necessary to . . .

la mesa	table
el platillo	dish (Mex)
el refresco	soft drink
la mantequilla	butter
el huevo	egg
la hamburguesa	hamburger
la tortilla	maize pancake (Mex)
el taco (Mex)	a tortilla with a filling
el aceite	oil
el azúcar	sugar
la salsa	sauce

picante	hot, peppery
frito	fried
asado	roast
a la parrilla	grilled

For more food vocabulary see pages 109–10.

ASI SE DICE

To say 'hello' when answering the phone:
¡Bueno!
To say who's speaking:
habla Verónica
To ask who's speaking:
¿de parte de quién?

To suggest an arrangement:
¿por qué no | nos vemos mañana?
| vamos al cine?
To ask if an arrangement is all right:
¿te/le/les parece bien?
or *¿qué te/le/les parece?*
or just *¿te/le/les parece?*

To ask if something would be possible:

¿podría | utilizar su teléfono?
| hablar más fuerte?
| repetirlo más despacio?
Note that *¿podría?* means 'could I . . .?' and 'could you/he/she?'

To apologise for something:
siento | llegar tan tarde
| no poder comer con usted

To ask how something is spelt:
¿cómo se escribe?

To say you've just done something:
acabo de | llegar
| hablar con el gerente

NOTAS DE LENGUA

¿Cómo se escribe?

The pronoun *se* has a number of uses in Spanish. As well as the reflexive use discussed in chapter 2, we have also seen it used in phrases like *se puede*, when it has an impersonal sense of 'one'. We would tend to say 'I', 'you', 'we' or 'they' in English depending on the context:

¿se puede estacionar aquí?	can I/we/you park here?
¿cómo se llega al centro?	how do I/we/you get to the centre?
se come muy tarde aquí	we/you/they eat very late here.

In these phrases the subject of the verb is not stated – it's a generalised, impersonal 'one'. But *se* is also used with a similar impersonal meaning when the verb does have a clearly stated subject:

se habla español	Spanish is spoken
se sirve el desayuno entre 7 y 10	breakfast is served between 7 and 10
¿cómo se pronuncia esta palabra?	how is this word pronounced?
¿cómo se escribe su apellido?	how is your surname written?

As you'd expect, when the subject is plural, the verb agrees:

| *se venden boletos aquí* | tickets are sold here |
| *se aceptan tarjetas de crédito* | credit cards are accepted |

¡Qué padre!

Conversations in Mexico are peppered with expressions of delight, enthusiasm, dismay etc. These are a few of the most common (there are many more vivid!):

¡qué padre!	how nice! great! (Mex)
¡qué pena!	what a shame!
¡qué lástima!	what a pity!
¡qué lindo!	how sweet (of you)! (Mex)
¡qué milagro!	fancy seeing you! (Mex)
¡qué horror!	how awful!
¡qué pesado!	how boring!

No future

In Spanish you will frequently hear the present tense used for actions in the near future:

te hablo a las 10	I'll call you at 10
en la nochecita te hablo	I'll ring you tonight
ahorita le suben su equipaje	they'll take up your luggage in a moment
nos vemos	I'll be seeing you
nos hablamos	I'll give you a call
estamos en contacto	we'll be in touch

Greetings

In Mexico, when friends meet they greet each other with:
¿qué hubo?
¿qué húbole?
¿qué pasó?
¿qué me cuentas?
as well as the expressions used in Spain such as:
¡hola!
¿qué tal?
¿cómo estás?
When saying goodbye over the phone, friends may say:
te mando un abrazo
te mando un beso (a kiss)
¡cuídate mucho! take care
¡qué estés bien! keep well
Hasta luego is used more frequently in Mexico than adiós, even in formal situations.

¡Bueno!

There are a number of useful words and phrases connected with making a phone call:

el conmutador	switchboard (Mex)
larga distancia	long-distance
por cobrar	reverse-charge (Mex)
con quien conteste	whoever replies
no contesta	there's no reply
la línea está ocupada	the line is busy
comunicar	to put through
(no) cuelgue	(don't) hang up
está equivocado/a de número	you've got the wrong number
no entra la llamada	I can't get through

Emiliano Zapata

LECTURAS

Tierra y libertad

Desde que comenzó a ser cultivado en Mesoamérica el maíz ha constituido el elemento básico de la dieta mexicana, ocupando un lugar central en religiones, leyendas y costumbres.

Hoy como antaño, la tortilla es el producto más típico derivado del maíz. Se puede tomar sola, y también es la base de unos 150 platos diferentes.

Actualmente, el maíz representa una parte muy importante de la producción agrícola de México, un país en donde tan sólo el 15% del suelo es cultivable. Tradicionalmente, esta tierra fértil ha sido propiedad de unos pocos y ricos latifundistas: la justa repartición de la tierra fue precisamente el objetivo principal de la revolución de 1910, uno de cuyos líderes fue el gran Emiliano Zapata. Hoy en día, en Morelos, su hijo Mateo continúa trabajando el campo, y recuerda a su padre con estas palabras: 'Para el pueblo, él representa un libertador. Para mí como hijo, él representa lo máximo de un padre'.

Emiliano Zapata, uno de los héroes con más carisma de la historia mexicana, fue asesinado en 1919. Los gobiernos posrevolucionarios han repartido más de la mitad de la tierra cultivable, pero la Reforma Agraria todavía no ha terminado. Como dice Saúl Ríos, de la Secretaría de Reforma Agraria, 'queda por alcanzar la soberanía alimentaria de nuestro país'.

1 What was the staple diet of the early cultures?
2 What importance did maize have amongst these peoples?
3 What was one of the major causes of the Revolution of 1910?
4 What has been done as regards land ownership since the Revolution?

Oro negro

El petróleo es el motor de la economía mexicana. Es el principal producto de exportación del país, y da trabajo a más de un millón de personas.

En el estado de Tabasco se encuentra la ciudad de Reforma, en donde se descubrieron nuevos yacimientos de petróleo a principios de los años setenta. La llegada de Pemex, la empresa paraestatal de petróleos, cambió totalmente el aspecto de la comunidad. Se construyeron clínicas, escuelas y un parque industrial, así como la primera carretera hacia el pueblo.

Cerca de Reforma se encuentra una de las mayores plantas petroquímicas del país, Cactus. La planta tiene como vecinos a los hermanos Ruiz, rancheros que se dedican a la actividad tradicional de Tabasco: la ganadería. La vecindad del rancho con Cactus plantea algunos problemas, el más grave de los cuales es el de la contaminación. La planta produce abundantes gases ácidos, y como dice Guillermo Ruiz: 'los alambrados se siguen destruyendo en seis meses . . . , hay una llovizna constante de petróleo aquí en el rancho'.

Los investigadores de Pemex vigilan regularmente el nivel de contaminación, y los hermanos Ruiz no son pesimistas acerca del futuro: 'Creo que es positivo lo que tenemos ya ahora. No quisiera volver yo a lo pasado,' dice Mariano Ruiz.

Pero quizás la presencia de Pemex no sea tan bienvenida en un futuro, si el problema de la contaminación no es resuelto.

1 When was oil discovered in Tabasco?
2 Has the oil boom brought any benefits to Reforma?
3 What are the drawbacks?
4 What is the reaction of the cattle-farmers?

EXTRA

A Ignacio is trying to phone Dr. Zamudio's surgery.

Voz:	¡Bueno!
Ignacio:	Buenas tardes. Con el Dr. Zamudio, por favor.
Voz:	¿A dónde quiere hablar?
Ignacio:	Al 511 39 34.
Voz:	Está equivocado.
Ignacio:	Disculpe.

Recepcionista:	¡Bueno!		
Ignacio:	¿A dónde hablo?		
Recepcionista:	Al consultorio del Dr. Zamudio.	**consultorio**	*surgery*
Ignacio:	Señorita, ¿podría darme cita con el doctor? Si es posible, me gustaría verlo pasado mañana.	**me gustaría**	*I'd like*
Recepcionista:	Muy bien. Venga sobre las 5 de la tarde. ¿Me da su nombre y su teléfono, por favor?	**pasado mañana**	*the day after tomorrow*
Ignacio:	Ignacio Pelayo, 514 59 65.	**sobre las 5**	*round about 5*
Recepcionista:	Bien. Queda confirmada la cita para el viernes a las 5.		

¿Verdad? Are these statements true or false?
1 Ignacio quiere una cita para el día siguiente.
2 Ignacio tiene que volver a llamar sobre las cinco de la tarde.

B Eva has problems when she tries to phone a friend.

Marcelo:	¡Bueno! ¡Bueno!		
Eva:	¿A dónde hablo?		
Marcelo:	A casa de la familia Reyna. Habla Marcelo.		
Eva:	Ay, Marcelo, no te reconocí la voz. La línea está malísima. Apenas te escucho.	**no te reconocí la voz**	*I didn't recognise your voice*
Marcelo:	Pues si quieres, cuelga, y yo te llamo. ¿Estás en tu casa?	**apenas**	*hardly*

Eva:	No, estoy en mi oficina. Te doy el nuevo teléfono.		
Marcelo:	Déjame apuntarlo . . . un momentito.	**apuntar**	*to take note/jot*
Eva:	605 11 49.		*down*
Marcelo:	¿Podrías repetirlo?		
Eva:	605 11 49.		
Marcelo:	En seguida te hablo.	**en seguida**	*immediately*

¿Verdad? 1 Marcelo quiere que Eva vuelva a llamar.
2 Eva está en su casa.

(sometimes synonymous with ahorita*!)*

C Héctor and Margarita are having lunch at Las Mercedes restaurant.

Héctor:	Buenas tardes, capitán. ¿Qué nos recomienda hoy?	**capitán**	*maître*
Capitán:	Pues . . . si les gusta el pescado, tenemos un exquisito blanco de Pátzcuaro. Si quieren comer carne, les recomiendo el cabrito al horno.	**blanco de Pátzcuaro**	*white fish from lake Pátzcuaro in Michoacán*
Margarita:	¿Y hay mole?		
Capitán:	Claro que sí, señorita. Es una de las especialidades de la casa.	**cabrito** **al horno**	*kid* *roasted*
Héctor:	A mí, se me antoja el pescado.	**sè me antoja**	*I feel like*
Margarita:	Y a mí, el mole.		
Capitán:	¿Y van a tomar una sopita, o les traemos unas botanas?	**botanas**	*appetisers*
Margarita:	Tengo mucha hambre. Voy a tomar la sopa de elote.	**sopa de elote**	*corn soup*
Héctor:	Yo prefiero unas crepas de huitlacoche. ¿Es la temporada, no?	**temporada**	*season*
Capitán:	Sí, señor. En seguida les servimos.		

¿Verdad? 1 Héctor y Margarita van a tomar unas botanas.
2 Héctor quiere comer el blanco de Pátzcuaro.

D Margarita Jiménez, who works for an import/export company, is trying to contact a potential customer.

Secretaria:	Buenas tardes. Oficina del Licenciado Valdés.		
Margarita:	Buenas tardes, señorita. Habla Margarita Jiménez, de Vendemex. Quisiera hablar con el Licenciado, por favor.	**quisiera . . .**	*I'd like*
Secretaria:	Su línea está ocupada, y hay otra persona que está esperando. ¿Podría volver a llamar más tarde, si es tan amable?		
Margarita:	Muy bien, hasta luego.		
	(Much later the same day.)		
Margarita:	Señorita, ¿el Licenciado Valdés sigue en su oficina?	**sigue**	*is still*
Secretaria:	Sí, señorita Jiménez. Ahorita le paso la llamada.		
Lic. Valdés:	¡Bueno!		
Margarita:	Buenas tardes, Licenciado. Habla Margarita Jiménez, de Vendemex.		

Lic. Valdés:	Muy buenas tardes. ¿Cómo está? ¿Recibió el catálogo?	**¿recibió...?**	*did you receive...?*
Margarita:	Sí, se lo agradezco mucho. Precisamente le hablo para decirle que nos interesa mucho trabajar con ustedes. ¿Cuándo nos vemos para hablar con más detalle?	**se lo agradezco** **con más detalle**	*thank you (for sending it)* *in more detail*
Lic. Valdés:	¿El próximo miércoles le parece bien? ¿Aquí en mi oficina, a las diez y media? Nosotros estamos muy interesados en incrementar las ventas al exterior; además, quiero que conozca a mi socio.	**incrementar** **las ventas al exterior** **quiero que conozca**	*increase* *sales abroad* *I want you to meet*
Margarita:	De acuerdo. Hasta el miércoles entonces.	**socio**	*partner*
Lic. Valdés:	¡Qué le vaya bien!		

¿Verdad?

1 La primera vez que Margarita llama, el Licenciado no se encuentra.
2 El Licenciado quiere vender sus productos en el extranjero.

MEXICO VIVO

Chocolate and chillies

Mexican cuisine is enormously varied and each state has its own specialities. The Spaniards were astounded by the splendid banquets of the Aztec ruler Moctezuma, not only because of the rich variety of ingredients but also the culinary skills of the Aztecs. From here, the Spaniards returned to Europe with chocolate, chillies, tomatoes, turkey, avocado pears, mint, peanuts and many other products. In fact the words we use for some of these foods come from the native Aztec ones.

But the Spanish also introduced products to Mexico: pork and chicken, garlic, vinegar and onions. Many of Mexico's best-known dishes are a synthesis of the two worlds. *El mole poblano*, often considered the national dish, combines chillies, chocolate and peanuts with almonds and sesame seeds from Europe.

What to order?

It is hard to single out dishes. Some favourites are: **chiles en nogada** served in August and September around the time of the Independence

Stall at Oaxaca market

celebrations. The peppers are stuffed with chopped pork and fruit, covered in a sauce of walnuts and cream, with a garnish of pomegranate seeds and parsley. The red, white and green colours of this dish are those of the national flag.

sopa de flor de calabaza pumpkin-blossom soup
tamales dumplings of cornmeal and chicken steamed in maize husks
pozole a stew-like soup of pork and corn
cabrito al horno roast kid
cochinita pibil spiced pork baked in banana leaves
ceviche raw fish marinated in lime juice
huachinango a la veracruzana red snapper in tomato sauce
crepas de huitlacoche/cuitlacoche pancakes stuffed with a black fungus grown on corn cobs

The **tortilla**, a maize pancake, is the basis of over one hundred different dishes, including the favourite fast foods of Mexico:

tacos tortillas with a filling
enchiladas tacos covered in a sauce. These are often served with grated salad and cheese, **guacamole,** a spicy avocado purée, and **frijoles refritos,** a purée of black beans.

Nos vemos tempranito

Working breakfasts are common in Mexico. Hotel restaurants can be crowded at 8 am and negotiations proceed over a fresh fruit juice, a healthy plate of assorted fresh fruits – melon, watermelon, banana, pineapple, mango and papaya – followed by a hearty dish of *chilaquiles*, fried *tortilla* strips cooked in a tomato, chilli, onion and cream sauce – reputedly good for a hang-over – or eggs prepared in countless ways – *huevos a la mexicana*, fried eggs with a tomato, onion and chilli sauce, *huevos rancheros*, the same but served with *tortillas*, *huevos ahogados* (drowned) in an even hotter sauce or *huevos norteños con machaca de Sonora* (dried beef).

¡Salud!

Tequila is the national drink: made from the heart of the blue agave cactus, it is taken with a pinch of salt and a wedge of lemon. The *margarita* cocktail is a combination of *tequila*, orange liqueur and lime juice, served in salt-rimmed glasses over crushed ice.

Though Mexico does produce some reasonable wine, it is far less popular than the Mexican beers – both dark, *oscura*, and light, *claro* – which are among the best in the world.

If you prefer to stick to soft drinks, *sidral* – a sparkling apple-flavoured drink – is a favourite. If you want mineral water, Tehuacán is the most famous Mexican brand.

If you order coffee, remember that *café con leche* tends to be milk with a dash of coffee: if you want it the other way round, ask for *café con crema. Café de olla* is a thick, sweet brew of coffee with cinnamon and sugar.

Sanborns

Sanborns is a chain of American-type drugstores where you can eat and also buy national and foreign magazines, books and gifts. They are open from breakfast until late. The most famous branch is in Calle de Madero, near the Zócalo in Mexico City. Once the home of a Spanish noble, it is called la Casa de los Azulejos because of the tiles covering the façade.

The Mexican economy

Mexico was first prized by the Spaniards for its gold and silver. Today, the country remains the world's largest silver producer and a leading producer of some other minerals. It ranks sixth in the world production of oil, which accounts for over a third of the country's revenue. The oil industry is run by the state-owned Petróleos Mexicanos, Pemex, who employ 180,000 workers and provide work directly or indirectly for 7% of the Mexican work-force.

Outside the area of petro-chemicals, manufactured goods represent 80% of Mexico's exports. Agriculture only accounts for 10%, although almost half the population works on the land. Despite its size, much of Mexico is unsuitable for cultivation.

PRACTICAS

Gaps

Fill in the gaps with items from the list below.

a ¿Cómo——su nombre?
b El restaurante——a la una, ¿no?
c El pollo——con papas francesas y ensalada.
d ——inglés en la zona turística.
e ¿——tarjetas de crédito?
f ¿Cómo——'¡qué padre!' en inglés?
g ——más de cincuenta lenguas indígenas en México.
h ¿——estampillas aquí?

se venden	se dice
se sirve	se pronuncia
se hablan	se aceptan
se habla	se abre

Matches

Match the questions with the answers.

a ¿Cuál es su dirección?
b ¿Dónde está su oficina?
c ¿A qué hora llega a la fábrica?
d ¿Tiene teléfono?
e ¿De parte de quién?
f ¿Cuándo nos vemos?
g ¿Es el 522 44 13?
h ¿Cómo se escribe?

1 *El fin de semana, si quieres*
2 *Sobre las 9.30*
3 *Con 's' al final*
4 *Río Nilo 50-B*
5 *En el cuarto piso de Comermex*
6 *Lo siento, está equivocado*
7 *Sí, es el 525 30 11*
8 *De la señora Moreno*

Over to you

You're on the phone. Say it in Spanish.

Voice: ¿Sí, bueno?
You: *Good morning. Is Leticia there?*
Voice: No, no se encuentra. Tiene clase.
You: *At what time could I call her?*
Voice: Después de las ocho.
You: *I can't call tonight.*
Could I leave a message?
Voice: Claro que sí. ¿De parte de quién?
You: *It's —. I'm very sorry but I can't see her tomorrow. I have to go to Toluca.*
Voice: Está bien. Le paso su recado.
You: *That's very kind. Goodbye.*

¡No me digas!

Choose the most likely response to the statements.

a El tránsito está muy pesado. Voy a tardar dos horas en llegar.
¡qué padre! ¡qué horror! ¡qué bonito!
b ¿Qué crees? Tengo muy buenas notas en mis exámenes.
¡felicidades! ¡qué lástima! ¡qué rico!
c Como mañana es tu cumpleaños te quiero invitar a comer.
¡qué caro! ¡buen provecho! ¡qué lindo eres!
d Desde el balcón, se ve todo el valle.
¡qué bonito! ¡qué pesado! ¡hasta la vista!
e Lo siento mucho pero no puedo venir esta noche.
¡qué lindo eres! ¡qué tal! ¡qué lástima!
f Mañana, te voy a presentar a mi colega.
¡qué bien! ¡mucho gusto! ¡encantado!

Pairs

Pair up the English with the corresponding phrase in Spanish.

a Don't hang up!
b Could you ring back?
c Speak louder, please!
d You've got the wrong number.
e The lines are busy.
f Who do you want to speak to?
g There's no reply.
h Could you repeat that?
i I'm putting you through.

1 *Las líneas están ocupadas.*
2 *¿Con quién quiere hablar?*
3 *¡No cuelgue!*
4 *No contestan.*

5 *¿Podría repetirlo?*
6 *Ahorita le comunico.*
7 *¿Podría llamar más tarde?*
8 *Está equivocado.*
9 *Hable más fuerte, por favor.*

¡Capitán!

Which dish would you recommend to the following people from the menu opposite?

a to Paulino, who is very keen on the cuisine of Acapulco
b to Ana, who is a strict vegetarian and wants something hot
c to Rogelio, who loves seafood and sauces
d to Patricia, who likes her fish grilled
e to Isabel, who wants a cold vegetable starter
f to Roberto, who is keen on mustard
g to Rosa, who wants pork
h to Luciano, who is allergic to seafood but wants some fish with garlic
i to Daniel, who loves beans

La línea está malísima

The secretary can only hear fragments of what the client says. Guess what the missing words are.

Lic. Carral: *¿Buenos días. ¿Se—el Sr. Sepúlveda?*
Secretaria: *Sí, pero su línea está ocupada. ¿Quiere esperar?*
Lic. Carral: *¿Sabe usted si—a tardar mucho?*
Secretaria: *Lo siento. No sé.*
Lic. Carral: *Entonces, ¿podría—un—?*
Secretaria: *¿Cómo no? ¿De parte de quién?*
Lic. Carral: *—Licenciado Carral. ¿Podría—si es— vernos mañana a las diez?*
Secretaria: *Con mucho gusto le paso su recado.*
Lic. Carral: *Muy—. —mañana.*

Answer back

Match the questions and answers.

a *¿Quieres ver la nueva película de Ripstein?*
b *¿Estás libre mañana en la tarde?*
c *¿Tienes compromiso el domingo?*

ESPECIALIDADES DE LA CASA

Cócteles

Ceviche acapulqueño
Cóctel de aguacate

Sopas

Sopa de verduras mixtas
Sopa especial
(pollo y arroz blanco)

Mariscos y pescados

Ostiones empanizados con salsa
tártara
Camarones mariposa
Filete de pescado a la parrilla,
empanizado o al mojo de ajo

Aves y carnes

Medio pollo a la parrilla con jitomate
y tocino
Filete de res con salsa mostaza
Puntas de filete a la ranchera

Platillos mexicanos

Enchiladas con frijoles
Tacos de cochinita pibil

d ¿Qué me recomiendas?
e ¿Te parece bien vernos a las 10?
f ¿Tienes mucha hambre?
g ¿Qué horas son?
h ¿Estás aquí en México?
i ¿A qué hora llega tu avión?

1 *No, te llamo desde Guadalajara.*
2 *A las 9.15, si no hay retraso.*
3 *Diez para las cinco.*
4 *Sí, tengo muchas ganas de verla.*
5 *Pues las enchiladas aquí están muy buenas.*
6 *Está bien, pero por favor no llegues tarde.*
7 *Mucha. Voy a ordenar dos platos.*
8 *No, no tengo nada que hacer.*
9 *No, tengo una cita con el dentista a las 6.*

Odd one out

With the help of the food list on pages 109–10 if necessary, find the odd one out.

a mango mantequilla plátano toronja
b piña papa papaya plátano
c taco enchilada mole tortilla
d zanahoria cebolla sandía lechuga
e refresco jugo cerveza hamburguesa
f hablar encontrar comunicar platicar
g llevar colgar marcar llamar

Out of order

Put this conversation with the hotel switchboard in sequence.

a Al 29 41 37.
b ¿A qué número?
c Quiero llamar larga distancia, por favor.
d En cuanto esté lista la llamada le aviso.
e Vuelvo a hablar más tarde. Gracias.
f A Mérida.
g No contestan.
h Buenas noches, a sus órdenes.
i ¿A dónde?

Crossed lines

Connect the bits of phrase on the left with those on the right, then put them in the correct order.

a ¿De parte	1 Jorge.
b Hola Jorge, soy Carmen. ¿Cómo	2 de quién, por favor?
c Está	3 a cenar. ¿Mañana puedes?
d ¿Te parece bien	4 has estado?
e Muy bien. Quiero invitarte	5 bien mañana. ¿A qué hora nos vemos?
f Habla	6 a las 6, en el Café Central?
g Buenos días. ¿Podría	7 mañana, entonces.
h ¡Perfecto! Hasta	8 hablar con Carmen?

¿Conoce usted México?

Say whether the statements are true or false.

a El chocolate es un producto introducido en México por los españoles.
b La bandera mexicana tiene los colores rojo, verde y blanco.
c El mole poblano es un animalito que se encuentra en el estado de Puebla.
d La margarita es un refresco.
e La expresión 'oro negro' significa petróleo.
f Emiliano Zapata fue el líder de la Independencia de México.
g Los chiles son los habitantes de un país sudamericano.
h La salsa ranchera no es picante.
i La tequila es el lugar donde se compran los boletos.

4 Para todos los gustos

Con dinero o sin dinero
hago siempre lo que quiero
y mi palabra es la ley.
No tengo trono ni reina,
ni nadie que me comprenda
pero sigo siendo el rey

(popular song)

EXPRESSING OPINIONS

DESCRIBING PEOPLE

LIKES AND DISLIKES

Mariachi band

EN DIRECTO

1 Patricia asked students about their television-viewing habits.

Patricia:	¿Ves mucho la tele?
Estudiante 1:	No, excepcionalmente.
Estudiante 2:	Poco, muy poco.
Estudiante 3:	No, no. No mucho.
Patricia:	¿Ves mucho la tele?
Estudiante 4:	Sí, me gusta mucho.
Patricia:	¿Qué tipos de programas te gustan más?
Estudiante 4:	Me gustan los deportivos, los de acción y los cómicos.
Estudiante 5:	Programas de acción, de aventuras.
Estudiante 6:	Programas especiales como musicales, culturales, noticieros.
Estudiante 7:	Deportivos, policíacos y cómicos.
Estudiante 8:	Los culturales, científicos . . . de todo veo un poco.
Estudiante 9:	Ah, la tele es más bien relajante, entonces lo que haya.

excepcionalmente — *rarely*

deportivos — *sports*
noticieros — *news/current affairs*
policíacos — *crime programmes*
científicos — *scientific*
más bien relajante — *kind of relaxing*
lo que haya — *whatever's on offer*

● **Spot-check 1** How many people mention comedy programmes?

Selections from Mexican tv

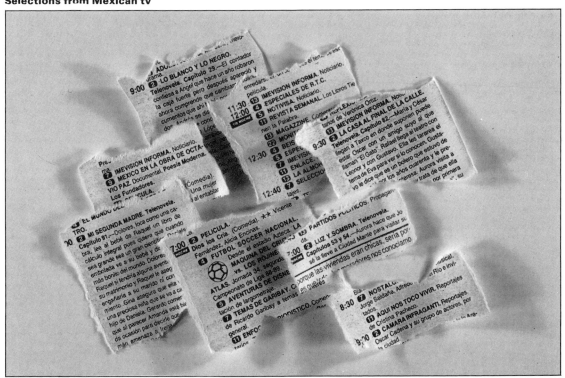

2   Patricia went on to ask what they thought about
telenovelas – the TV soaps which attract vast
audiences.

Patricia:	¿Y qué opinas de las telenovelas?		
Estudiante 1:	Irreales, aburridas. No me gustan.	**irreales**	*unreal*
Estudiante 2:	Definitivamente aburridas. No me gustan.	**aburridas**	*boring*
Estudiante 3:	Bueno, pues son irreales y a veces son muy	**a veces**	*sometimes*
	dramáticas.	**algunas**	*some*
Estudiante 4:	Pues hay algunas buenas y otras malas, pero en	**otras**	*others*
	general no . . . no me gustan mucho . . . que digamos.	**que digamos**	*so to speak*
Patricia:	¿Y qué opinas de las telenovelas?	**jamás**	*never*
Estudiante 5:	Jamás veo una. No me gustan mucho las telenovelas.	**no tienen**	*they are very*
	Me parece que no tienen ninguna calidad.	**ninguna**	*poor*
		calidad	

● **Spot-check 2**   How many people like *telenovelas*?

┌───┐
To ask someone's opinion of something:
¿qué opina(s) de . . .?
To say what you think:
me parece que │ **es aburrido**
                  │ **son interesantes**
└───┘

3   Patricia asked people to describe their ideal partner.

Patricia:	¿Cómo es tu pareja ideal?	**pareja**	*partner*
Estudiante 1:	Alto, trigueño, guapo.	**alto**	*tall*
Estudiante 2:	Me gusta que sea cariñosa, que sea dulce y que sea	**trigueño**	*fair* (Mex)
	muy inteligente.	**guapo**	*handsome*
Estudiante 3:	Físicamente, que sea alto, guapo, fornido . . . pues, el	**me gusta que**	*I like her to*
	hombre perfecto.	**sea . . .**	*be . . .*
Estudiante 4:	Mayor que yo, inteligente, que no sea feo.	**cariñosa**	*affectionate*
Estudiante 5:	No sé. Puede ser cualquier mujer inteligente y guapa	**dulce**	*sweet*
	. . . no sé.	**físicamente**	*physically*
Patricia:	Y tú, ¿serías una pareja ideal?	**fornido**	*strong/well*
Estudiante 5:	Supongo que sí. No sé.		*built*
Patricia:	Y tú, ¿serías una pareja ideal?	**mayor**	*older*
Estudiante 6:	Yo pienso que sí porque soy agradable, simpático.	**feo**	*ugly*
Estudiante 3:	Soy agradable, simpática . . . bueno, depende	**cualquier**	*any*
	también de los hombres, ¿no?	**¿serías . . .?**	*would you*
Estudiante 2:	Bueno, yo me considero la pareja ideal, pero, pues		*be . . .?*
	eso depende de las mujeres.	**agradable**	*pleasant*
		simpático	*nice*

● **Spot-check 3**   How many people think intelligence is an important
quality?

depende de	*it depends on*

> *To say you agree:*
> **pienso** | **que sí** *I think so*
> **creo** |
> **supongo que sí** *I suppose so*

Let's be fair
Trigueño, from *trigo*, corn, is an uncommon word for 'fair-haired' or 'fair-skinned'. The more usual expression in Mexico is *güero/a*, frequently used as a form of address in the diminutive, *güerita*. Fair people in Mexico are assumed to be from the United States. It must be remembered that whereas in English 'America' refers almost exclusively to the U.S.A., in Spanish it applies to Latin America: 'De América soy hijo, y a ella me debo' (José Martí). The Spanish words to describe people from the U.S. are *estadounidense* and *norteamericano*; more colloquial and a little pejorative is the term *gringo*.

4 We all have to get out of doing things at times. What excuses do people give?

Patricia:	Si alguien te invita a salir y no quieres, ¿qué excusa le das?	**alguien**	*someone*
Estudiante 1:	Ay . . . me duele la cabeza.		
Estudiante 2:	Que tengo dolor de . . . no, que tengo mucho trabajo.		
Estudiante 3:	Que tengo mucha tarea.	**tarea**	*homework* (Mex)
Estudiante 4:	Que tengo otras cosas que hacer.	**tengo . . . que hacer**	*I have . . . to do*
Estudiante 5:	Pues diría que estoy ocupado, que estoy estudiando.		
Estudiante 6:	Pues le digo que tengo otro compromiso o que voy a un museo . . . generalmente, se echan a correr.	**diría** **museo**	*I'd say* *museum*
Estudiante 7:	Que no tengo tiempo. Depende también quien me invite.	**se echan a correr**	*they run away*
Estudiante 8:	Le digo que hay una mala influencia planetaria.	**hay una mala influencia planetaria**	*the stars are against it*
Patricia:	Si alguien te invita a salir y no quieres ¿qué excusa le das?		
Estudiante 9:	Pues, le digo la verdad, de que no quiero salir.		

● **Spot-check 4** How many people actually say they don't want to go out?

To tell the truth
¿Verdad? on its own means 'that's so, isn't it?'
If you are stating a fact, you can say:
es verdad que . . .
es cierto que . . .

VOCABULARIO

la fiesta	party, festival
el baile	dance
guapo/a	handsome
feo/a	ugly
simpático/a	nice, friendly
mayor	older
alto/a	tall
bajo/a	short
gordo/a	fat
delgado/a	thin
moreno/a	dark (-haired/-skinned)
rubio/a	fair (-haired/-skinned)
inteligente	intelligent
agradable	pleasant
contento/a	happy
triste	sad
aburrido/a	boring
interesante	interesting
mejor	better
peor	worse
creer	to think, believe
opinar	to think (have an opinion)
tener razón	to be right
tener ganas de	to feel like
saber	to know
importar	to matter
divertirse	to enjoy oneself
depende (de)	it depends (on)
otro/a	other
alguien	someone
algún/alguna	any
ningún/ninguna	none, no
nunca	never
siempre	always
a veces	sometimes
nadie	no-one
también	also
tampoco	neither

ASI SE DICE

To ask someone's opinion:
¿qué | opina(s) | (de) . . .?
       | piensa(s) |

To give your opinion:
pienso |
    creo | que . . .
me parece |
en mi opinión, . . .
para mí, . . .
In Mexico, you can also say:
se me hace que . . .

To say you agree:
pienso |
    creo | que sí   I think so
me parece |
estoy de acuerdo   I agree
tiene razón   you're right
supongo que sí   I suppose so

To disagree:
pienso |
    creo | que no
me parece |

To say you feel like doing something, use
tener ganas de:
¿tienes ganas de ver la película?
no, no tengo ganas
sí, tengo muchas ganas
In Mexico, you can also say:
¿se te antoja ir al cine?
sí, se me antoja mucho

NOTAS DE LENGUA

Negatives

The words for 'nothing', 'no-one' and 'never' in
Spanish are nada, nadie and nunca.

nada importa	nothing matters
nadie contesta	nobody is answering
nunca me escribe	he never writes to me

Often they come after a verb, in which case the verb
is preceded by no:

no hace nada	he doesn't do anything
no conozco a nadie	I don't know anyone
no canta nunca	he never sings

The negatives can be combined:

no vemos nunca a nadie	we never see anyone
or even	
nadie nunca ve nada	(Work it out!)

Jamás is a slightly more emphatic way of saying
nunca:
jamás veo las telenovelas

También . . . tampoco

También means 'too', 'also', 'as well':
me gusta también la música pop I also like pop music
In the negative, *también* becomes *tampoco*:
no me gusta tampoco la música pop I don't like pop
music either
As with *nada, nunca,* and *nadie, tampoco* can also go
before the verb. In this case, the *no* is dropped:
tampoco me gusta la música pop

También and *tampoco* can be used to agree with
someone:
Me gustan los mariachis.
A mí también. So do I.
No me gustan los mariachis.
A mí tampoco. Neither do I.

Neither . . . nor

Use the form *ni . . . ni . . .*:
ni Pablo ni Alfonso pueden venir neither Pablo nor
Alfonso can come
no me gustan ni la radio ni la televisión I don't like
radio or television

But

Normally, 'but' is translated as *pero* in Spanish:
quiero hablar con el Lic. Reyes pero no se encuentra
I want to speak to Lic. Reyes but he's not here
If you are making a negative statement where two
objects, actions or ideas are contrasted, *sino* replaces
pero:
*No quiero hablar con la Lic. Marrón sino con el Lic.
Reyes* I don't want to speak to Lic. Marrón but to Lic.
Reyes
No fui a Huatulco sino a Puerto Angel I didn't go to
Huatulco but to Puerto Angel

Something or other

i *Algo* means 'something' or 'anything':

¿quieres tomar algo? do you want something to
drink/eat?

ii To say 'someone', 'anyone' the word is *alguien*:
¿hay alguien en la oficina? is there anyone in the
office?
¿conoces a alguien de la Facultad? do you know
anybody in the Faculty?

iii To say 'some' in the sense of 'some or other', the
adjective to use is *algún/alguna/algunos/algunas*:
espero verla algún día I hope to see her some day
¿hay alguna parada de autobús por aquí? is there
any bus stop around here?
todavía quedan algunos asientos de no fumar
there are still some no-smoking seats left
algunas personas nunca saben lo que quieren
some people never know what they want

iv The negative of *algún* is *ningún*:
no queda ningún asiento there aren't any seats left
no hay ninguna parada por aquí there aren't any
stops near here

Know-how

In Spanish there are two main verbs meaning 'to
know' – *conocer* and *saber*.
Conocer means to know a person or place. 'To know'
in this context has the sense of 'to be acquainted
with':
¿conoces México?
conoce a mucha gente
Saber means
i to know a fact, a language etc.:
¿sabes italiano?
no sé a qué hora sale el avión
ii to know how to do something – usually expressed
as 'can' in English:
¿sabes nadar?   can you swim?
no sé manejar   I can't drive

Comparing

Expressing opinions may well involve comparing.
Simply put *más* or *menos* before the adjective and
que after it:

es **más** bonito **que** Acapulco it's prettier than Acapulco

eres **más** inteligente **que** tu hermana you are more intelligent than your sister

es **menos** interesante **que** la otra película it's less interesting than the other film

To say the bigg**est**, tall**est** etc.:
la ciudad **más** grande
la persona **más** alta
la novela **más** interesante

Note that some adjectives in Spanish contain the idea of comparison, so don't need *más* or *menos* in front of them: *mayor* older, *mejor* better, *peor* worse.
Patricia es mayor que yo Patricia is older than me
el clima es peor que en Inglaterra the climate is worse than in England

Ser or estar?

Adjectives can be used with the verbs *ser* or *estar*.

If they are describing what a person or thing is like, the verb to use is *ser*:
soy alto
Guillermo es simpático
mi coche es rojo

If the adjective is describing a person's mood, health or any other non-permanent state, the verb to use is *estar*:
estoy muy contenta
¿cómo estás?
la puerta está abierta

Some adjectives can be used with both *ser* and *estar* depending on the context:

Rosa es aburrida	Rosa is a boring person
Rosa está aburrida	Rosa is bored

LECTURAS

Una clase de danza

Gloria Contreras es la figura máxima de la danza contemporánea en México. La danza tiene una larga tradición en el país, pero cursos de baile contemporáneo, como los que dirige Gloria en la Universidad Autónoma Nacional de México, son inusuales.

Actualmente, Gloria tiene más de trescientos alumnos y, con una sola excepción, ninguno de ellos es profesional. A pesar de sus otras actividades, dedican largas horas a perfeccionar sus técnicas. Para Susan Schinkel, una de las estudiantes, 'El momento de la danza es un momento de recogimiento . . . de tranquilidad, por la cual sacas todas tus tensiones'.

Otro de los estudiantes es Roberto Quintana, el único hombre de la clase. Por ser varón, ha tenido que vencer muchos prejuicios para dedicarse a la danza: 'La familia mexicana no deja que los hijos, sobre todo los varones, se dediquen a este tipo de actividades'.

En este momento, el grupo ensaya una danza mexicana, 'Sensemayá', del compositor Silvestre Revueltas. Es una evocación del pasado prehispánico de México.

A pesar del éxito del curso, su futuro no está asegurado, debido a la crisis económica que sufre el país. Gloria, sin embargo, no es pesimista: 'Espero que, a pesar de la crisis, nosotros podamos seguir rindiendo y probando que la danza mexicana también tiene un lugar en el mundo'.

1 How many of Gloria's students are professional?
2 Why is it more difficult for men to take part?
3 Why is the future of the classes uncertain?

La cultura mexicana, según Carlos Fuentes

Carlos Fuentes es uno de los escritores e intelectuales más conocidos del México de hoy en día. Entre sus obras más importantes se encuentran 'La región más transparente' y 'La muerte de Artemio Cruz'. A él le preguntamos cómo afecta a México su vecindad con un país tan poderoso como los Estados Unidos. Esta fue su respuesta:

'México, que es un país que mantiene viva una cultura indígena, una memoria de su pasado indígena, una memoria de su pasado español, europeo, medieval, mediterráneo, es un país que está dispuesto a ir hacia delante pero sin sacrificar su pasado. Esto para mí es un hecho fundamental sobre México, es un hecho esencial que caracteriza al país y que le da un valor fundamental, sobre todo en su situación fronteriza, de ser frontera con los Estados Unidos, pero no sólo frontera mexicana, sino frontera latinoamericana al mismo tiempo.

México y la América Latina están teniendo una influencia cada vez mayor en los Estados Unidos, a través de su literatura, a través de su música, a través de la realidad política de nuestros países, a través de la presencia de tantísimas personas de origen hispano-americano en todos los Estadcs Unidos. Y son portadores de valores culturales muy importantes, y a veces de valores culturales que se han perdido en los Estados Unidos.'

Carlos Fuentes

1 What is Mexico's attitude towards its past?
2 What do you understand by the expression *situación fronteriza*?
3 In which areas is Mexican culture having an impact in the United States?

EXTRA

A Margarita and Héctor are discussing plans for the weekend.

Margarita: Oye, Héctor, nos han invitado a una fiesta en casa de los Durán el sábado. ¿Tienes ganas de ir?

Héctor: Realmente, no me gustan las fiestas. ¿Por qué no vamos a ver la película que ponen en el cine Elektra?

Margarita: ¿Cuál es?

Héctor: 'Frida' – la historia de la pintora Frida Kahlo.

Margarita: Ay, ¿no te acuerdas? La ví hace mucho pero no me importa verla otra vez. Siempre me ha fascinado su obra – me parece una mujer extraordinaria. Creo que he visitado su casa en Coyoacán por lo menos cinco veces.

Héctor: Yo nunca he ido. Realmente sé muy poco de ella; por eso me interesa ver la película.

Margarita: Sí merece la pena – es muy original.

Héctor: Entonces, ¿me acompañas al cine el sábado?

Margarita: Sí, y el domingo te llevo a Coyoacán.

¿Verdad? Are these statements true or false?
1 Héctor tiene muchas ganas de ir a la fiesta.
2 Margarita no conoce la casa de Frida Kahlo.

nos han invitado	we've been invited
ponen	they're showing
pintora	painter
¿no te acuerdas?	don't you remember?
ví	I saw
hace mucho	a long time ago
me ha fascinado	has fascinated me
su obra	her work
he visitado	I've visited
por lo menos	at least
yo nunca he ido	I've never been
por eso	for this reason
me interesa ver	I'm interested in seeing
merece la pena	it's worth it
¿me acompañas...?	will you come with me...?

B Carlos has been trying to get some theatre tickets – without success.

Carlos: Elena, habla Carlos.

Elena: Hola, Carlos. ¿Qué pasó?

Carlos: ¿Qué crees? Que ya no quedan boletos para el teatro mañana.

Elena: ¡No me digas! ¡Qué pena! Lo dejamos para la próxima semana, ¿no?

¡no me digas!   *don't tell me!*

Carlos: Muy bien. Pero si quieres, puedo preguntar si hay boletos para el concierto de Tania Libertad en el Auditorio. Se me antoja salir mañana.

concierto   *concert*

Elena: Andale, pues. Háblame mañana en la tardecita.

ándale (coll)   *go on*

Carlos: De acuerdo. Hasta luego.

Elena: Hasta luego. Y gracias.

¿Verdad? Carlos y Elena van al teatro mañana.

C Angeles and Guillermo are talking about what they do in their spare time.

Angeles: Jamás me aburro en el D.F. Hay tantas cosas que hacer. Hay buen teatro, buenos conciertos y como mi pasión es la lectura voy muy seguido a las presentaciones de nuevas publicaciones en la librería del Sótano. Puedes hacerles preguntas a los escritores y escuchar las opiniones de otras gentes.

jamás me aburro   *I never get bored*
tantas   *so many*
lectura   *reading*
muy seguido (Mex)   *very often*

Guillermo: Entre semana me levanto muy temprano y voy al gimnasio. Soy fanático del ejercicio. Los sábados voy a correr en el Bosque de Chapultepec, después me gusta nadar y tomar el sol. En la noche salgo con mis cuates. Los domingos no hago nada especial – más bien descanso, veo un video, como y duermo . . .

librería   *bookshop*
escritores   *writers*
otras gentes   *other people*
gimnasio   *gymnasium*
correr   *to run*
mis cuates (coll. Mex)   *my friends*
más bien descanso   *mostly I rest*

¿Verdad?
1 Angeles es fanática del cine.
2 Guillermo va al gimnasio todos los días.

MEXICO VIVO

Sonidos de México

Music played an important part in the ceremonies of the Mayas, Mixtecs, Aztecs, Zapotecs and other indigenous peoples. To their wind and percussion instruments, the Spaniards added strings and brass. As Mexico has so many peoples and cultures, each region has its own 'sound'. For example, the *marimba* (a sort of xylophone) is typical of Oaxaca, Chiapas and Tabasco; the accordion is the basis of *la música norteña* (northern music); along the Gulf coast you can hear Afro-Cuban influences in the *sones jarochos*; and Jalisco is home of *mariachi* music – the inimitable combination of trumpets, violins and guitars. The music was first played at weddings, but now it has come to be regarded as 'typically' Mexican, and is played at *fiestas* and receptions, in hotel bars and restaurants. The *bolero* is also very popular in Mexico, as is *la música ranchera*, a type of 'country and western': one of the greatest exponents was Chavela Vargas. Inevitably, *la música pop* has had a great impact on younger generations but traditonal music still has many fans and bands playing *la música tropical* in the dance-halls offer spirited and colourful competition to hard rock.

Dance

People may have heard of the Mexican 'hat dance', *el jarabe tapatío*, but are probably unaware of the rich variety of rhythms and costume in regional folk-dancing in Mexico. Many of these dances are rooted in ancient rituals, for example the 'deer dance', *la Danza del Venado*, of the Yaqui Indians of Sonora, or the flying-pole dance from Papantla, Veracruz. Others date back to the Conquest: *'los moros'*, a re-enactment of the battle between Moors and Christians in Spain, is still widely performed in central Mexico. An evening with the Ballet Folklórico de México at the Bellas Artes theatre in Mexico City is a very enjoyable way of becoming acquainted with Mexico's dances and music.

Fiestas

The Mexican calendar is punctuated with religious festivals and holidays. It is said that between 5,000 and 6,000 are celebrated throughout the country each year. Apart from Christmas and Easter, the most important date in the calendar is Independence day, *el Grito*. At 11 pm on September 15, the President of Mexico begins celebrations with the cry (*el grito*) *¡Viva México!* It was this cry which signalled the start of Father Hidalgo's rebellion against Spanish rule in 1810 and heralded the beginning of the Independence movement. Celebrations continue throughout the 16th – particularly in Mexico City and Guanajuato. Another uniquely Mexican festival, a fusion of Catholic and indigenous beliefs, is *el Día de los Muertos* (November 1 and 2). October 12 is *el Día de la Raza* marking the emergence of the *mestizo* race; December 12 is the day of *Nuestra Señora de Guadalupe*, patroness of Mexico. Some of the liveliest and most colourful fiestas are: *Carnaval* (Lent) in Veracruz and Mazatlán; *la Feria de San Marcos* (April) in Aguascalientes; and *Lunes del Cerro* (July) in Oaxaca.

La charrería

The horse was a source of wonderment and consternation for the Indian peoples at the time of the Conquest. During the colonial period, only Spaniards were allowed to ride horse-back as a mark of their status, but the spread of cattle-ranching gave birth to the *charro* (cowboy), a skilled horseman and consummate artist with the lasso. The *charro* is much more flamboyant than his Wild West counterpart, and even today his traditional values are summed up in the motto of the Charros de Jalisco: 'Patria, Mujer y Caballo'. *Charreadas* (rodeos) still attract large crowds in the D.F. and Guadalajara, and throughout north-west Mexico. *La charrería* came to be recognised as a national sport. Of course nowadays football has a massive following, and tennis, boxing, baseball and the martial arts are very popular – but, unlike *charreadas*, they're not accompanied by *mariachis*!

Modern art in Mexico

Frida Kahlo, the painter mentioned in the first 'Extra' dialogue, is one of Mexico's many famous twentieth-century artists. She was married to Diego Rivera, the muralist, and the house where they lived in Coyoacán, in the south of Mexico City, is open to the public. Her work can also be seen in the Museo de Arte Moderno, where the variety of styles in modern Mexican art can be appreciated. It includes two muralists' easel work, along with paintings by Leonora Carrington, Raul Anguiano, Pedro and Rafael Coronel, José Luis Cuevas and Rufino Tamayo.

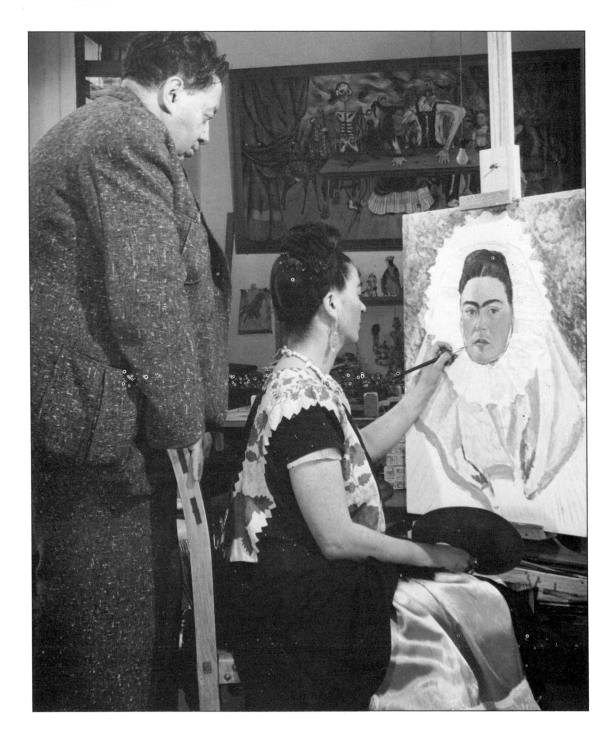

PRACTICAS

Say it in Spanish

a I suppose so.
b I don't agree.
c You're right (*tú*).
d It depends on the weather.
e She doesn't feel like going.
f What do you think of the film?
g I never eat hamburgers.
h I don't know anyone.
i This restaurant is better than the other one.

Blanco y negro

Match up the pairs of opposites.

guapo	ocupado
nunca	ningún
alto	detrás
todos	feo
también	bajar
subir	nadie
delante	tampoco
algún	bajo
libre	divertido
aburrido	siempre

Gaps

Fill the gaps with one of the following words; only one is correct in each case.

sino, pero, también, tampoco, ni . . . ni . . .

a Sí, la música clásica me gusta, — prefiero el pop.
b Es sábado, — no tengo ganas de salir a bailar.
c No voy a ir a Ixtapa — a Puerto Vallarta.
d Soy como mi padre. A mí me gustan los deportes, a él —.
e No me gusta Pedro Infante y — José Alfredo Jiménez.
f Sí, me gusta la televisión y — el cine.
g No quiero ir al parque y — a Xochimilco.
h No habla — francés — alemán.

Over to you

You're discussing a mutual friend. Say it in Spanish.

Tomás: ¿Conoces al hermano de Jorge?
You: *Yes, I know him quite well.*
Tomás: Y ¿cómo es?
You: *He's very pleasant and very intelligent.*
Tomás: Es mayor que Jorge ¿no?
You: *Yes, he's twenty-four.*
Tomás: ¿Y se parece a él?
You: *No, he looks like their father, and he's much taller than Jorge.*
Tomás: Y ¿te cae bien?
You: *Yes, I think he's very nice.*

Do you know?

Fill in the gaps with the correct form of the verbs *saber* or *conocer*.

a ¿ — usted si el camión va a tardar mucho?
b No, nosotros no — Cuernavaca.
c ¿Cómo — (tú) que Alicia no va a venir?
d Necesito — si puedo hacer una reservación.
e No, yo no — a Julio César, pero ya — que es muy buena persona.
f Tengo muchas ganas de — al presidente.
g ¿Ya — cuándo va a tomar las vacaciones?
h ¿ — (tú) el último libro de Elena Poniatowska?

Answer back

Pair up the following questions and answers.

1 ¿Qué te parece la comida?
2 ¿Conoces al hermano de Lupita?
3 ¿Cómo te va en el nuevo trabajo?
4 ¿Qué piensas de la música de Juan Gabriel?
5 ¿Cómo son las clases de la Universidad?
6 ¿Qué te parece la ciudad?

a *Algunas interesantes, otras aburridas.*
b *Sólo me gusta escucharla de vez en cuando.*
c *Sí, se parece mucho a ella.*
d *Fascinante, hay tantas cosas para ver.*
e *Estupenda, la carne está muy rica.*
f *Bastante bien, aunque el jefe es un poco machista.*

Frida Kahlo and Diego Rivera

Cóctel de letras

The letters in these words, which all appear in the *Vocabulario*, have been shaken up; sort them out and ¡salud!

a SAMCITIPO
b GANUNIN
c POIRAN
d ADIBURRO
e POGUA
f EDAIN

A matter of opinion

All these verbs are used to express feelings and opinions. Fill the gaps with the correct form for each of them.

parecer, opinar, creer, preferir, gustar

a ¿Qué te — mis nuevos zapatos?
b ¿Qué — tú, carne o pescado?
c A mí, lo que más me — es la música pop.
d Yo — que voy a tomar un poco más de pescado.
e ¿Le — bien vernos mañana?
f Yo — viajar en avión a Acapulco.
g A mí, me — que va a llover esta tarde.
h ¿Qué — del nuevo libro de Paz?
i Beatriz, te — mucho a tu papá.
j Sí, el cine me —, pero la verdad es que — el teatro.

La vida es cruel

Here is an extract from what could be a popular *telenovela*. Fill the gaps with the correct word.

algún, algunas, alguien, nadie, ningún, ninguna

Dolores: Estoy muy sola en este mundo. — me comprende.
Mari-Luz: ¡Qué cosas dices, Dolores!
Dolores: — mañanas, cuando me levanto, me siento muy triste. Luego hablo con — colega en el trabajo y ya me siento mejor. Pero fíjate, no tengo amigos. No tengo — amiga de verdad.
Mari-Luz: ¿Y qué son Pepa y Lucita sino amigas?
Dolores: Sí, de acuerdo, pero con — de ellas puedo platicar a gusto. De verdad, necesito a — que esté a todas horas cerca de mí.

Mari-Luz: ¡Con lo pesada que eres, no creo que lo encuentres!

About people

Look at the following statements and decide which adjective suits the person described.

1 No quiere ver la televisión, no quiere ir a bailar, no quiere hacer nada.
   a *simpática*   b *interesante*   c *aburrida*

2 ¡Se parece tanto a Paul Newman!
   a *moreno*   b *gordo*   c *guapo*

3 Joaquín tiene tres años más que yo.
   a *alto*   b *mayor*   c *menor*

4 Me van a llevar primero al cine, después a cenar y más tarde, a bailar.
   a *feos*   b *simpáticos*   c *delgados*

5 Clara ya no sale conmigo, así que no lo estoy pasando muy bien últimamente.
   a *contento*   b *mayor*   c *triste*

6 Está así porque le encantan los postres.
   a *moreno*   b *gordo*   c *divertido*

¿Conoce usted México?

Are the following statements true or false?

a Los charros son músicos que tocan música ranchera.
b Los instrumentos tradicionales de los mariachis son la guitarra, la trompeta y el violín.
c La marimba es un pez tropical que se encuentra en el Golfo de México.
d El Grito es la canción más popular entre los jóvenes mexicanos.
e Nuestra Señora de Guadalupe es la patrona de México.
f Las telenovelas son programas noticieros.
g El jarabe tapatío es un refresco muy dulce.

5 Pasado y futuro

> Que no caigan en la bajada ni en la
> subida del camino. Que no encuentren
> obstáculos ni detrás ni delante de ellos,
> ni cosa que los golpee.
> Concédelos buenos caminos,
> hermosos caminos planos.
>
> Popol Vuh

HIRING A CAR
GETTING THINGS REPAIRED

EN DIRECTO

1 In Cancún, Martha Santos wants to explore the region by car.

Dependienta: Buenos días.

Martha: Buenos días, señorita. Quiero rentar un auto pequeño para dos días.

Dependienta: A ver (*looking at list*). Sí, tenemos un Topaz automático pero no tiene aire acondicionado.

Martha: ¿Cuánto cuesta por día?

Dependienta: Son noventa mil pesos por día, más quinientos sesenta por kilómetro. O con kilometraje ilimitado son ciento setenta y cinco mil pesos por día. Los seguros y el impuesto no están incluidos.

Martha: Está bien. ¿Es posible devolverlo en el aeropuerto de Mérida?

Dependienta: Sí, pero tiene que pagar un cargo extra de doscientos treinta mil pesos.

Martha: De acuerdo. Voy a pagar con tarjeta de crédito.

Dependienta: Muy bien. ¿Me da su licencia, por favor? (*Martha hands over her driving licence.*) Gracias.

dependienta	*employee*
rentar (Mex)	*to hire*
auto	*car*
a ver	*let's see*
por día	*per day*
más	*plus*
kilometraje ilimitado	*unlimited mileage*
seguros	*insurance*
impuesto	*tax*
incluidos	*included*
devolverlo	*return it*
cargo extra	*extra charge*

● **Spot-check 1** 1 Are taxes included in the price quoted?

2 Where does Martha want to return the car?

To ask *if something is possible:*
¿es posible?
¿es posible devolverlo en el aeropuerto?

Returns only

Devolver is used for returning things:
¿cuándo me devuelves el dinero? when are you
going to give me the money back?
Volver is used when people are returning:
¿cuándo vuelves a México? when are you coming
back to Mexico?

Taxing

El impuesto means any sort of tax. In this dialogue it
refers to value added tax. In Mexico, this is *impuesto
al valor agregado* or *IVA.*

2 Victoria César goes to a photographic shop to get her
camera repaired.

Victoria:	Buenas tardes.
Dependiente:	Buenas tardes.
Victoria:	Señor, mi cámara no funciona. ¿Me la podría reparar?
Dependiente:	A ver . . . (*He examines the camera.*) ¿No necesita una pila nueva?
Victoria:	No. Acabo de cambiarla.
Dependiente:	Bueno. La voy a checar. (*He writes out a receipt.*) ¿Su nombre, por favor?
Victoria:	Victoria César.
Dependiente:	(*Handing over the ticket*) Aquí tiene.
Victoria:	¿Cuándo puedo recogerla?
Dependiente:	Pues, pasado mañana por la mañana, dependiendo de lo que pueda tener.
Victoria:	¡Ay! ¿No podría hacerlo más rápido?
Dependiente:	No, lo siento. Tengo mucho trabajo.
Victoria:	Bueno. Muchas gracias. Hasta luego.
Dependiente:	Hasta luego.

¿no necesita? *perhaps it needs*
pila *battery*
nueva *new*
checar *have a look*

recoger *collect, pick up*
dependiendo *depending on*
de lo que *what's wrong*
pueda tener
más rápido *quicker*

● **Spot-check 2** 1 Does the camera need a new battery?

2 When can Victoria collect the camera?

> To say something doesn't work:
>
> | mi cámara | no funciona |
> |---|---|
> | el elevador | |
>
> To ask if something could be repaired:
> **¿me la/lo podría reparar?**

> To ask when you can collect something:
> **¿cuándo puedo recogerla/lo?**

Rápido

In Spanish, adjectives are frequently used as adverbs to describe an action:

¡qué lindo canta Silvia!	how nicely Sylvia sings!
Pepe maneja muy lento	Pepe drives very slowly
¿lo podría hacer más	could you do it more
rápido?	quickly?

3 At the travel desk of a Cancún hotel, Alejandro Montano finds out about excursions along the coast.

Alejandro:	Buenos días, señorita.
Empleada:	Buenos días.
Alejandro:	¿Me podría recomendar alguna excursión a la costa?
Empleada:	Sí. Le recomiendo que visite Tulum. Es un sitio arqueológico muy bonito y muy interesante.
Alejandro:	¿Hay alguna playa cercana?
Empleada:	Sí, a quince minutos hay una playa magnífica en Akumal. Si quiere, puede bucear en el arrecife.
Alejandro:	¿Y puedo rentar equipo ahí?
Empleada:	Sí, claro. Aquí tiene un folleto con toda la información de las excursiones en la costa.
Alejandro:	Muy amable. Gracias.
Empleada:	De nada.

recomendar	*recommend*
costa	*coast*
que visite	*that you visit*
sitio	*archaeological*
arqueológico	*site*
cercana	*nearby*
magnífica	*magnificent*
bucear	*skin-dive*
arrecife	*coral reef*
equipo	*equipment*
folleto	*leaflet*

● **Spot-check 3** 1 What can you do at Akumal?
2 What information is contained in the leaflet?

4 On the beach at Akumal, Alejandro goes into the Dive Shop to hire some equipment.

Alejandro:	Buenos días.
Dependiente:	Buenos días.
Alejandro:	Me gustaría rentar un visor, un esnórkel y unas aletas.
Dependiente:	Sí, claro. Son quince mil pesos diarios y tiene que dejar un depósito de cincuenta mil pesos. Pero si

visor	*mask*
esnórkel	*snorkel*
aletas	*flippers*
diarios	*per day*
depósito	*deposit*

The Mayan site of Tulum on the Caribbean coast

	quiere ver el arrecife, es mucho mejor bucear con tanques.	**tanques**	*cylinders*
Alejandro:	Pero no tengo experiencia.		
Dependiente:	No es problema. Ofrecemos un curso para principiantes. Dura un día y cuesta ciento cuarenta mil pesos.	**ofrecemos** **curso** **principiantes**	*we do/offer* *course* *beginners*
Alejandro:	¿El equipo está incluido?		
Dependiente:	Sí.		
Alejandro:	¿Y lo puedo tomar hoy mismo?		
Dependiente:	Sí, claro. ¿Quiere llenar esta forma, por favor?	**llenar**	*fill in*

● **Spot-check 4**   1 How much deposit is payable?
  2 How long is the beginners' course?

> *To say what you'd like (to do):*
> **me gustaría (rentar un visor)**

Me gustaría

Me gustaría means 'I should like', both as a request and when expressing a personal wish:
me gustaría bucear en el arrecife
me gustaría pasar unos días en Cozumel
Remember, if you are asking someone what they would like, the pronouns must change accordingly:
¿te gustaría visitar Uxmal? would you (*tú*) like to visit Uxmal?
¿les gustaría tomar algo? would you (*ustedes*) like to have something to drink?

preguntar	*to ask*
necesitar	*to need*
funcionar	*to work (function)*
devolver	*to return (an object)*
recoger	*to collect, pick up*
rentar (Mex)	*to hire*
revisar	*to check, look over*
reparar	*to repair*
lavar	*to wash*
limpiar	*to clean*
planchar	*to iron*

VOCABULARIO

la cámara	*camera*
la pila	*battery*
la batería	*car-battery*
el depósito	*deposit*
el seguro	*insurance*
el impuesto	*tax*
la licencia	*driving licence* (Mex)
el curso	*course*
la costa	*coast*
la excursión	*excursion*
el folleto	*leaflet*
la ropa	*clothes*
la lavandería	*laundry*
el coche	*car*
el taller	*repair garage, workshop*

(For car vocabulary see page 111)

el equipo	*equipment*
el reloj	*watch*
la cocina	*kitchen*
el cuarto de baño	*bathroom*
la recámara (Mex)	*bedroom*
la cama	*bed*
los muebles	*furniture*

(For more vocabulary relating to living accommodation see page 111)

el problema	*problem*
descompuesto/a	*not working* (Mex)
roto/a	*broken*
listo/a	*ready*
incluido/a	*included*
por día	*per day*

ASI SE DICE

To say something doesn't work:
mi cámara | no funciona
el elevador |

To ask if something can be repaired:
¿me la/lo/las/los podría | reparar?
| arreglar?

To ask when you can collect something:
¿cuándo puedo recogerla/lo/las/los?
To ask when something will be ready:
¿cuándo estará lista/o?

To ask if something is possible:
¿es posible?
¿es posible devolverlo en el aeropuerto?
¿es posible pagar con tarjeta de crédito?

To say what you'd like to do:
me gustaría | bucear
| rentar un coche

NOTAS DE LENGUA

Para-phernalia

Para has many uses, including:
i   to say whom something is intended for:
    un regalo para ti
    un curso para principiantes
ii to say what something is intended for – either a destination:
    un boleto para Cancún

or a purpose:

te hablo para invitarte a comer

¿qué se hace para conservarlo?

planes para un cinturón turístico

iii   to refer to the future:

un auto para el mes de septiembre

¿para cuándo necesita la cámara?

para el próximo miércoles

Por ejemplo

Some uses of *por* have already been seen:

i   meaning 'along' or 'through':

siga por esta calle

hay que pasar por aquella puerta

ii   meaning 'around':

¿vive usted por aquí?

por esta colonia hay muchos cines

iii   meaning 'per':

¿cuánto cuesta por día/hora?

iv   in set phrases like:

por favor   please

por ejemplo   for example

por supuesto   of course

It has many other uses, including:

v   'by' in the sense of authorship:

una novela escrita por Juan Rulfo

vi   'times' in the sense of multiplication:

dos por dos son cuatro

Not working

If something isn't working, you can say:

no funciona

no sirve

anda mal

está descompuesto (Mex) (for anything mechanical)

If it's broken:

está roto/a

If it's jammed:

está atorado/a (Mex)

If you want someone to have a look at something that's not working:

¿podría revisarlo/la?

or *¿podría echarle un vistazo?*

You will also hear *checar*, one of a number of anglicisms used in Mexico (though considering the proximity of the U.S., there are relatively few of them, except in the north).

Getting things fixed

When you need to get something fixed, these are some of the places to go:

el taller mecánico/de coches	repair garage
la zapatería	shoe shop
la relojería	watch-repair shop
la óptica	optician's
la tintorería	dry cleaner
la lavandería	laundry/launderette
la peluquería	hairdresser

For other specialist services you may need, see page 112.

LECTURAS

La magia de los mayas

Palenque es uno de los más importantes centros arqueológicos mayas. Situado en el límite de la selva tropical, hace 1.300 años era una gran ciudad, con una extensión de 12 kilómetros cuadrados. Hoy en día, lo único que se ve es el centro; la mayor parte de la ciudad queda todavía por excavar.

Tras su declive, Palenque permaneció escondido hasta el siglo XVIII, cuando sus ruinas fueron descubiertas. En 1949, el arqueólogo Alberto Ruz hizo un descubrimiento espectacular. Tras cuatro años de excavaciones, encontró la cripta funeraria del gobernante más importante de Palenque, Escudo Solar. No se ha encontrado ninguna otra pirámide maya construida especialmente para contener una tumba.

Actualmente, la arqueóloga responsable de las investigaciones es Rosalba Nieto. Ahora mismo, está trabajando en un mapa que registra todas las construcciones de la ciudad. Su mayor preocupación es la conservación de las ruinas: 'La selva y la lluvia constantes van destruyendo poco a poco los edificios . . . Ahora procuramos ya no excavar, sino tratar de conservar lo que hemos excavado.'

Para Rosalba, Palenque 'es un sitio muy, muy especial. La primera ocasión que estuve aquí, sentí algo mágico. Día con día, sientes algo diferente, algo que no sientes en cualquier otro sitio. Quizás se deba a la grandeza de la selva, a la grandeza de los mayas.'

1 What was Palenque like 1,300 years ago?
2 What spectacular discovery was made in 1949?
3 What is Rosalba working on at the moment?
4 What are the main threats to the preservation of Palenque?

El arrecife de coral

Cada año, miles de turistas llegan a Cancún, en busca de las vacaciones perfectas. Hace 20 años, la ciudad era tan sólo un brazo de arena; hoy en día, es un centro turístico internacional, que continúa creciendo a un ritmo acelerado.

Una de las grandes atracciones para los visitantes es el arrecife coralino, uno de los más importantes del

Rosalba Nieto

Templo de las Inscripciones, Palenque

mundo. Los corales son organismos sensibles, muy vulnerables a la presencia humana. El biólogo Eric Jordán, que se dedica a su estudio, afirma que el turismo 'afecta directamente al arrecife a través de contactos físicos, de romper cosas, de matar peces, de tomar recuerdos'.

Los turistas pueden destruir un arrecife en cuestión de pocos años. Es por ello que algunos profesores de buceo, como Alberto Friscione, han decidido incorporar un mensaje ecológico en sus clases. Alberto dice a los estudiantes: 'les suplico no tocar nada, no romper y sobre todo, no traer recuerdos con ustedes'.

Aunque la industria turística ejerce una presión continua sobre el delicado ecosistema, la muerte del arrecife en un futuro todavía puede evitarse, si se toman las medidas necesarias. Según Eric Jordán, el equilibrio entre el turismo y la preservación de los arrecifes coralinos es 'perfectamente posible'. El arrecife 'puede seguir siendo una fuente muy importante como recurso económico'.

1 How has Cancún changed in the last 20 years?
2 What do the tourists do to the reef?
3 What are some diving instructors doing to help protect the reef?

EXTRA

A Lupita is considering renting a self-catering apartment – *una suite*.

Lupita:	Buenos días, señor.
Portero:	Buenos días, señorita. ¿En qué puedo ayudarle?
Lupita:	Les hablé por teléfono para preguntar los precios de sus suites, que me parecen muy bien, y ahora me gustaría ver una de ellas si es posible.
Portero:	Sí, con mucho gusto. Déjeme ver . . . la 502 no está ocupada. El problema es que tenemos que subir por las escaleras: el elevador no funciona.
Lupita:	No importa, ¡es buen ejercicio!
	(*They reach the flat.*)
Portero:	Pase usted, señorita. Como ve, tiene una sala bastante amplia, una recámara con teléfono y un clóset muy grande. Y aquí está el baño, con tina y regadera . . . Y la cocina, chiquita pero que tiene de todo: refrigerador, estufa, vajilla.

portero	*hall porter*
les hablé por teléfono	*I phoned you*
por las escaleras	*by the stairs*
ejercicio	*exercise*
sala	*sitting-room*
amplia	*large, spacious*
clóset (Mex)	*wardrobe*
tina	*bath*
chiquita	*small*
de todo	*everything*
estufa (Mex)	*cooker*
vajilla	*china*

Lupita:	¿Y hay servicio de limpieza y lavandería?	**limpieza**	*cleaning*
Portero:	Sí, señorita. Y a la vuelta de la esquina, usted tiene el mercado y el súper.	**lavandería**	*laundry*
		a la vuelta de	*around*
Lupita:	¡Estupendo! Me gustaría hacer una reservación para la próxima semana.	**súper = supermercado**	
		¡estupendo!	*great!*
Portero:	Entonces vamos a bajar y le tomo sus datos.	**sus datos**	*your details*

¿Verdad? Are these statements true or false?

1 La suite tiene dos recámaras.
2 Lupita quiere hacer una reservación para la semana siguiente.

B Margo is having trouble with her car and takes it to the garage – *el taller*.

Margo:	Buenos días.		
Mecánico:	Buenos días.	**motor**	*engine*
Margo:	¿Podría revisar mi coche, por favor? El motor se calienta mucho y no arranca.	**se calienta mucho**	*is overheating*
		no arranca	*it doesn't start*
Mecánico:	Bueno, vamos a echar un vistazo. ¿Quiere abrir el cofre, por favor? (*Margo opens the bonnet.*) Sí, mire. La banda está rota.	**echar un vistazo**	*have a look*
		cofre	*bonnet*
Margo:	¿Cuánto tiempo va a tardar en reparar el auto?	**banda**	*fan-belt*
Mecánico:	Dos horas, más o menos.	**llanta ponchada** (Mex)	*a flat tyre*
Margo:	Está bien. Tengo una llanta ponchada en la cajuela. ¿Podría arreglarla al mismo tiempo?	**cajuela** (Mex)	*boot*
		arreglarla	*fix it*
Mecánico:	Por supuesto.	**al mismo tiempo**	*at the same time*
Margo:	Muchas gracias. Muy amable.		

¿Verdad?

1 El motor se calienta porque el cofre está cerrado.
2 El mecánico va a reparar más de una cosa.

C Carlos wants to know how he can get some clothes cleaned at his hotel.

Recepcionista:	Buenos días, señor. ¿En qué puedo servirle?		
Carlos:	Tengo unas camisas para lavar y planchar. ¿Hay servicio de lavandería?		
Recepcionista:	Claro que sí. Tiene que meter la ropa en la bolsa de plástico que está en su habitación y llenar la forma. Deje la bolsa en su cama y llame a la lavandería, marcando el 1.	**meter**	*put*
Carlos:	¿La tendrán lista para esta tarde?	**¿la tendrán lista...?**	*will they have it ready...?*
Recepcionista:	(*Looking at watch*) Pues sí, en la tarde, alrededor de las siete.	**alrededor de**	*around*
Carlos:	Perfecto. Gracias.		

¿Verdad?

1 Hay que meterse en la cama con la bolsa antes de llamar a la lavandería.
2 La ropa va a estar lista al otro día.

MEXICO VIVO

The Yucatán peninsula

The Yucatán peninsula – the horn of Mexico between the Gulf and the Caribbean – comprises the states of Campeche, Yucatán and Quintana Roo. The landscape ranges from thick jungle, where ocelots and jaguars may still be found, to sisal plantations, scrub vegetation, beaches of powder-fine sand and forests where the sapodilla tree thrives, providing latex from which chewing-gum is made. Chewing *chicle* was a prehistoric habit – and some may say that it still is.

For a long time the peninsula was a land apart. The Maya offered fierce resistance to the Spaniards and the spirit of rebellion persisted throughout the colonial period. The geographical isolation fostered separatist tendencies – for a time the Yucatán broke away from the rest of the Republic, and the bitter Caste War in the nineteenth-century took thousands of lives.

Economic prosperity (for the land-owning aristocracy) brought stability towards the end of the last century, and the demand for *henequén*, to make rope, produced great wealth, as can be seen in the magnificent mansions in Mérida built by an elite who had more contact with Europe than with the rest of Mexico.

Improvements in communications and the creation of Cancún as an international holiday resort have opened up the region to make it one of Mexico's main tourist attractions. Because it was isolated, the area has preserved a peculiar charm; the people are courteous and gentle, the cuisine unique. There is concern that the influx of tourists, beneficial to the economy and the creation of jobs, should not upset the ecological balance or destroy the unique character of the region.

Caribbean coral

One of the great attractions of the Caribbean coast is its coral. The most famous reef is el Arrecife del Palancar which starts at the island of Cozumel and stretches down to Belize. It is the second largest reef in the world and is now protected by the Mexican government under its status as a major nature reserve – *reserva de la biósfera*.

The area has attracted professional divers for some years. The first centres were at Akumal and Cozumel, a small island just off the coast considered one of the finest places in the world for diving. With its 50 dive shops, Cozumel is a mecca for amateurs as well as professionals. But the totally inexperienced can glimpse some of the delights of the underwater world at Xel-Ha, a beautiful lagoon on the mainland a few miles from Tulum. Because of its popularity, a major problem to the survival of delicate marine life here is sun-tan oil.

Mexico's coast

Mexico has over 6,000 miles of coastline; 4,500 miles are on the Pacific, which has attracted tourists for many years.

In the north, the Sea of Cortés, between the Baja California peninsula and the mainland, offers sheltered waters and excellent fishing at resorts like La Paz, Loreto, Bahía Kino, Guaymas and Los Cabos.

The southern part of the Pacific Coast is famous for the beauty of its lush tropical mountains and fine sandy bays. Acapulco's importance goes back to the sixteenth century, when the Spanish established it as their trading port with the Far East; today, it is a large tourist resort of nearly one million inhabitants. Most other centres along the coast have only developed in the last few decades. Puerto Vallarta was the first, after the film 'Night of the Iguana' brought it to public eyes in the 60s. The most recent centres are Ixtapa, Puerto Escondido, Puerto Angel and Huatulco.

The Gulf coast, while not as spectacular as the Caribbean or the Pacific, does offer two big centres renowned for fishing at Tampico and Veracruz, the port founded by Cortés when he landed at the start of the Conquest.

Ancient Mexico

The many indigenous groups of Mexico's past have

left an exceptional number of archaeological sites. In 1988 there were 13,500 officially documented sites and more are found each year.

The most distinctive feature of many major sites is the pyramids, which have temples on top; unlike in Egypt, these pyramids do not usually contain tombs. Some of the larger sites also have a ball-court where a ritual ball-game, *el juego de pelota*, was played. At the end of the contest the winning side was sacrificed. Spaniards had never seen rubber balls before, and when they took them back to Europe they probably laid the foundation for all modern ball games.

The best introduction to the enormous wealth of sites and artefacts is the magnificent **Museo**

Nacional de Antropología in Mexico City, considered by many to be one of the world's greatest museums. Mexico City has the most important Aztec site – the **Templo Mayor** – and also the site of the great market of **Tlatelolco** at the **Plaza de las Tres Culturas**. Within a hundred miles of the city are a large number of other sites, including **Teotihuacán**, the most important city in ancient Mesoamerica, and **Tula**, capital of the Toltecs and famous for its gigantic statues sitting atop the main pyramid. South of Mexico City, the state of Oaxaca contains the impressive site of **Monte Albán**, the Zapotec capital, and **Mitla**, a smaller Mixtec site famous for its beautiful stone mosaic friezes.

On the Gulf coast north of Veracruz is **El Tajín**, once

Puerto Vallarta, a popular resort on the Pacific coast

home of the Huastecs and now still used by the Totonac Indians for their ritual flying pole-dance. Further south is one of the oldest sites in Mexico, **La Venta**, dating back to 1200 BC and home of the Olmecs. The site itself is in the middle of a swamp and many finds (or replicas of them) are displayed in the **Parque Museo de la Venta** in Villahermosa, where you can admire the famous basalt heads with distinctly negroid features which still puzzle archaeologists.

Near Villahermosa on the edge of the tropical rain-forest is **Palenque**, the Mayan site said to be the most beautiful in Mexico; other famous Mayan sites are at **Uxmal** and **Chichén Itzá**.

The Maya

The Maya are one of the most fascinating and longest surviving of the ancient civilizations. No-one can fail to be moved by the sight of Tulum perched on the cliffs above the turquoise waters of the Caribbean, or Palenque set against the verdant backdrop of the rain-forest of northern Chiapas. Mayan history probably goes back 2,000 years to the jungles of Central America; subsequently their influence extended from the Pacific coast to the Gulf of Mexico and the shores of the Caribbean. On the flat limestone plain of the Yucatán peninsula, hundreds of cities flourished. Many sites have been explored, but many more will probably remain buried in the rain-forests for ever. Uxmal, with its exquisite filigree stone-carvings, and the grandeur of Chichén Itzá, a fusion of Toltec and Mayan cultures, bear witness to the architectural skills of a people who were also expert mathematicians, astrologers and astronomers. Charting the course of the stars and planets with extreme precision, the Maya devised a solar calendar of 365.2422 days.

Pyramid of the Sun at Teotihuacán

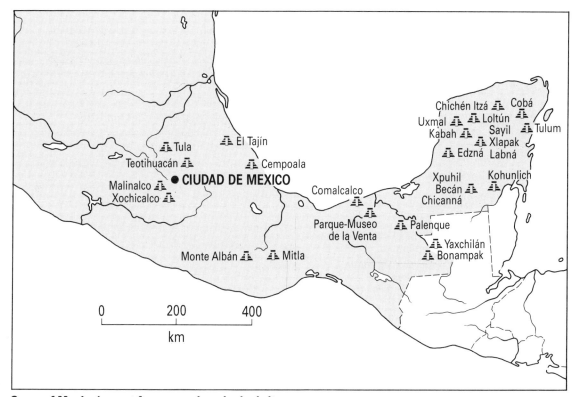

Some of Mexico's most famous archaeological sites

PRACTICAS

Say it in Spanish

a   I'd like to go to Mérida.
b   When can I collect the car?
c   How much does it cost per day?
d   I need a new battery.
e   Could you recommend me a good restaurant?
f   When are you (*tú*) going back to London?
g   Is it possible to change my ticket?
h   I'd like to have breakfast in my room.
i   How long will you take to mend it?

¿Por o para?

Choose the right word to fill the gaps.

a   ¿— cuándo va a estar lista la ropa, — favor?
b   Pase usted — aquí.
c   El curso — principiantes empieza mañana.
d   — ir a Chapultepec, tome el colectivo.
e   El Támesis pasa — Londres.
f   ¿Cuándo nos vemos — comer?
g   Sólo quedan dos semanas — Navidad.
h   Siete — siete son cuarenta y nueve.
i   ¿Podría dejar un recado — Alicia?
j   Nos van a cobrar 10.000 pesos — hora.

On the road

You go to a car hire office. Say it in Spanish.

You:	*Good afternoon. I'd like to hire a small car.*
Empleada:	¿Para cuándo lo quiere?
You:	*Today, if it's possible.*

Empleada:	Sí, no hay problema. ¿Para cuánto tiempo lo necesita?
You:	*For five days – until Saturday.*
Empleada:	Muy bien. Pues aquí tiene un folleto con toda la información.
You:	*Thank you. I'd like to know if I could leave it at Mérida airport, or do I have to return it here?*
Empleada:	No, no es necesario. Puede dejarlo en el aeropuerto pero hay un cargo extra.
You:	*Is the insurance included in the price?*
Empleada:	No, no están incluidos. Ni el impuesto tampoco.
You:	*The small cars don't have air conditioning, do they?*
Empleada:	No – y le advierto que hace muchísimo calor en esta temporada.
You:	*Then I would like to hire a bigger car – but not too expensive.*
Empleada:	Está bien. El Coral le sale muy económico y es mucho más cómodo. Le va a gustar.

Help

Each person below needs help. From the list underneath, choose the appropriate place for them to go:

a No, no funciona. Necesita una pila nueva.
b Tengo que ir a recogerlas cuanto antes: no veo nada sin ellos.
c No puedo caminar más con ellos: tengo que arreglármelos.
d Se ha ponchado la llanta otra vez.
e Hay que lavar estas camisas.

*la lavandería, la óptica, la relojería,
el taller mecánico, la zapatería.*

Se compra, se vende

Read the advertisements and decide which place is best suited to the people below.

a En el centro de la ciudad, departamento ideal para solteros. Una recámara, cocina y terraza.
b ¡Oportunidad única! Magnífica mansión en San Angel. 8 recámaras, 4 baños, biblioteca, estudio, jardín de 2.000 m², garaje para cinco coches; alberca.
c A estrenar, piso de dos recámaras en Polanco. Cuarto piso con mucha luz, amplia cocina. Jardín comunitario.
d Casa en la colonia Florida. 90 m². Una recámara, sala, cocina chiquita pero con todos los electrodomésticos incluidos. La casa se puede alquilar con muebles o sin ellos.
e Se renta recámara amueblada. Señorita honorable. Todos los servicios.

1 *Rosario is an air hostess, lives alone and wants to rent a room.*
2 *Juan and Esperanza are both bank employees. They want a place where their two small children can play safely outdoors.*
3 *Pepe wants a compact but fully furnished house.*
4 *Sergio is looking for a place where he can keep his four Rolls-Royces safely.*
5 *Esteban loves going out every night of the week.*

No hay problema

You've got problems. Say it in Spanish to the hotel receptionist.

You:	*Hello. My shower isn't working. Is it possible to mend it this afternoon?*
Recepcionista:	Lo siento mucho, pero hoy no puede ser.
You:	*Well, I would like to change rooms.*
Recepcionista:	Pues espere un momentito. Voy a ver si tenemos una habitación libre.
You:	*Thank you. I have also got some clothes to be washed. Is there a laundry here?*
Recepcionista:	Sí. Hay que llamar al número 06.
You:	*Do you know when the clothes will be ready?*
Recepcionista:	Mañana en la mañana.
You:	*But I need them for tonight.*
Recepcionista:	No se preocupe. Seguro que lo podemos arreglar.

Car hire

Answer the questions by studying the extracts from the hire car contract below.

a How old is Señor Figueroa?
b When does his driving licence expire?
c In which district of Mexico City does he live?
d What is the post code of his office?
e What position does he hold in the company?
f How many days has he rented the car for?
g Did he take out all insurances?
h When was the car handed back?

¿Conoce usted México?

Are the following statements true or false?

a En muchos sitios arqueológicos de México, hay pirámides.
b El motor de un coche deja de funcionar cuando el chicle se rompe.
c Acapulco está en el Golfo de México.
d México tiene el segundo arrecife coralino más importante del mundo.
e Una selva es un tipo de camisa bordada hecha por los mayas.
f Es posible que el fútbol derive del juego de pelota practicado en México.
g En la península yucateca hay poca vegetación.

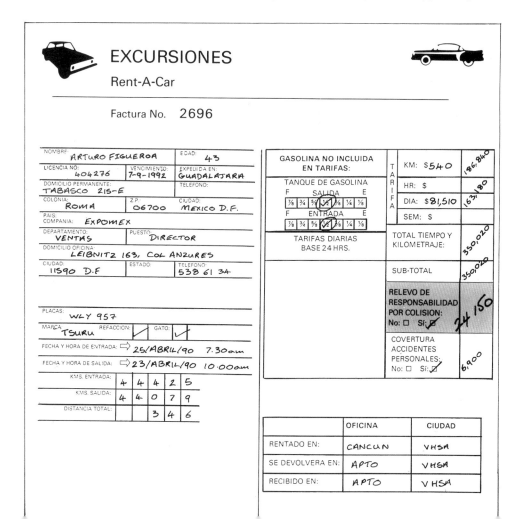

Grammar revision

ESPAÑA VIVA

As **México Vivo** is designed to follow on from **España Viva**, it assumes a knowledge of certain words, phrases and basic grammar covered in the earlier course. This is a summary of the main grammar points.

NOUNS

In Spanish, as in English, a noun is a word that tells you what something or someone is: *una ciudad* (a city), *una mujer* (a woman), *un coche* (a car).

Gender
In Spanish every noun has a gender, either feminine or masculine: *chica* (girl) and *cerveza* (beer) are both feminine; *chico* (boy) and *tomate* (tomato) are masculine.

As a general rule, words ending in *-a* are feminine and those ending in *-o* are masculine. Of course there are exceptions: *mano* (hand) is feminine, *mapa* (map) is masculine. And there are some words that end in letters other than *-a* and *-o*: *leche* (milk) – feminine, *pastel* (cake) – masculine.

Articles
There are two words for 'a' – *una* and *un*. You use *una* with feminine nouns, *un* with masculine nouns.

Similarly, there are two words for 'the' – *la* and *el*, depending on the gender of the noun: **la** *chica,* **la** *cerveza,* but **el** *chico,* **el** *tomate.*

Note that if the words *a* or *de* come before *el*, the two words run together: **al** *lado* **del** *banco.*

In Spanish the definite article *la* or *el* is used when talking about things in general, whereas in English it isn't:
no me gusta la cerveza   I don't like beer
juego al fútbol   I play football

Plurals
When there are two or more of something, it's called a plural. There are two simple rules for making a noun plural in Spanish:

1 If it ends in a vowel, simply add *-s*:
   una patata   *tres patatas*
   un kilo   *dos kilos*
2 If it ends in a consonant, add *-es*:
   una mujer   *dos mujeres*
   un hotel   *cinco hoteles*

Before a plural noun, the word for 'the' changes from *la* or *el* to *las* or *los*:
las *chicas*   (feminine noun)
los *chicos*   (masculine noun)

The plural form of the indefinite article is used to mean 'a few', 'some':
¿quiere unas aceitunas?   would you like some olives?

ADJECTIVES

An adjective describes people, places or things. It normally goes next to a noun:
un vestido **rojo**   a **red** dress

or after 'is' or 'are':
este vestido es **bonito**   this dress is **pretty**

Position
In English, when an adjective and a noun come together, the adjective comes first, eg 'a **small** loaf'. In Spanish the adjective usually follows the noun:
una bolsa **grande**   a large bag
los zapatos **rojos**   the red shoes

Agreement
Adjectives have to 'agree' with nouns they describe. They usually have four possible forms: feminine singular and plural, and masculine singular and plural:

una camisa **roja**	a red shirt	(fem. sing.)
un coche **rojo**	a red car	(masc. sing.)
dos camisas **rojas**	two red shirts	(fem. pl.)
dos coches **rojos**	two red cars	(masc. pl.)

The endings are usually similar to the ending of the noun they describe; adjectives which don't end in -o or -a have only one singular and one plural form:

una chaqueta **gris**, un pantalón **gris**	a grey jacket, a pair of grey trousers
unas chaquetas **grises**, unos pantalones **grises**	some grey jackets, some pairs of grey trousers
una manzana **verde**, un melón **verde**	a green apple, a green melon
unas manzanas **verdes**, unos melones **verdes**	some green apples, some green melons

Adjectives of nationality that don't end in -o/-a behave slightly differently, in that they **do** change in the feminine:

un chico **español**	una chica **española**
un coche **inglés**	una bicicleta **inglesa**

When an adjective describes any mixtures of masculine and feminine nouns, it's used in the masculine plural:

María y José son españoles
el pan y la fruta son muy baratos

(See also POSSESSIVES and DEMONSTRATIVES below.)

A way of making an adjective more forceful is to add -ísimo or -ísima to the end:

una comida buena	a good lunch
una cena **buenísima**	a really good dinner

Possessives
Possessive adjectives are 'my', 'your', 'his', 'her' etc:

mi	my
tu	your (informal)
su	your (formal); his, her, its
nuestro/a	our
vuestro/a	your (informal, plural)
su	your (formal, plural); their

Because they're adjectives, they agree with the noun they go with:

mi hermano	my brother
mis hermanos	my brothers

su coche	his car (or her car or their car)
sus coches	his cars (or her cars or their cars)

The English **'s** (apostrophe **s**) doesn't exist in Spanish. Instead you have to turn the words around and use *de* (of):

los hijos de mi amigo	my friend's children
la casa de Alfonso	Alfonso's house

Demonstratives
The words for 'this' and 'that' can be either adjectives or pronouns. There is one word for 'this' and two for 'that' in Spanish. One of the words for 'that' refers to something very recent or close to you, the other to something distant in time or place.

As **adjectives**, all these words agree with the noun they describe. The different words are shown in these examples:

this	*esta camisa, este plato, estas camisas, estos platos*
that (close)	*esa camisa, ese plato, esas camisas, esos platos*
that (distant)	*aquella camisa, aquel plato, aquellas camisas, aquellos platos*

As **pronouns**, meaning 'this one' or 'that one', they may be written with an accent: *ésta, ésa, aquélla.*

When the gender of the thing hasn't been established, *esto* and *eso* are used without an accent: *¿qué es esto?, eso es todo.*

PRONOUNS

These are the 'shorthand' way of referring to people (or things): 'I', 'you', 'he', 'she', etc.

Subject pronouns
These are the subject of a verb – '**I** go', '**she** lived', '**we** are arriving':

yo	I	
tú	you (informal, singular)	
usted*	you (formal, singular)	(* *usted* and
ella	she	*ustedes* are
él	he	often short-
nosotros/as	we	ened in
vosotros/as	you (informal, plural)	writing to
ustedes*	you (formal, plural)	*Ud* and *Uds*)
ellos/as	they	

Notes:

1   Having learnt these pronouns, the next thing to do is to remember not to use them all the time! Very often, the ending of the verb (see VERBS below) will tell you who is being referred to. For example:
    ¿dónde vives? means 'where do you live?' – *tú* is not necessary as *vives* can only refer to *tú*.

2   The word for 'it' is, technically, *ella* (for a feminine thing) or *él* (for a masculine thing), but in practice these words are rarely used as subject pronouns.

Pronouns with *gustar*

The pronouns to use with the verb *gustar* are *me, te, le, nos, os, les*:

me gusta el español	I like Spanish ('Spanish pleases me')
le gustan los espárragos	he likes asparagus ('asparagus pleases him')
nos gusta el fútbol	we like football ('football pleases us')

QUESTIONS

One way of asking a question is to put a question word at the front, eg:

¿cómo?	how?	*¿qué?*	what?
¿cuándo?	when?	*¿cuál?*	which?
¿dónde?	where?	*¿quién?*	who?
¿adónde?	where (to)?	*¿cuánto?*	how much?
¿por qué?	why?	*¿cuántos/as?*	how many?

When you use these interrogatives, the subject (if there is one) comes after the verb:
*¿cuántos hijos tiene **usted**?*
*¿dónde está **el hotel**?*
*¿cuál es **su profesión**?*
*¿a qué hora sale **el tren**?*

If the question doesn't begin with an interrogative, you can raise the tone of your voice to turn a statement into a question:

Enrique tiene dos coches   *¿Enrique tiene dos coches?*

Or you can make a statement and check that it's true by adding *¿no?* or *¿verdad?* at the end:

Enrique tiene dos coches, ¿verdad?

You can also reverse the order of the subject (if there is one) and the verb:
¿tiene Enrique dos coches?

VERBS

Spanish verbs are listed in dictionaries in their infinitive form, eg *trabajar* – to work, *tener* – to have, *vivir* – to live. Each verb has a number of different forms, and the form used depends on a number of factors. The three most important ones are:

1   Which category is the verb in? Does the infinitive end in *-ar*, *-er* or *-ir*? (Each of these groups has a slightly different pattern.) Or is the verb in question an 'irregular', which breaks the rules at some point?

2   Is the action in the present, the past or the future? In other words, what 'tense' is it in? The present is the main one used in *España Viva*.

3   Who is performing the action? Who is the 'subject' – I, you, she etc?

Verb patterns in the present tense

A   REGULAR VERBS

1   *-ar* verbs, eg *trabajar* (to work)

yo	trabaj**o**	nosotros/as	trabaj**amos**
tú	trabaj**as**	vosotros/as	trabaj**áis**
usted } él, ella }	trabaj**a**	ustedes } ellos/as }	trabaj**an**

2   *-er* verbs, eg *comer* (to eat, have lunch)

yo	com**o**	nosotros/as	com**emos**
tú	com**es**	vosotros/as	com**éis**
usted } él, ella }	com**e**	ustedes } ellos/as }	com**en**

3   *-ir* verbs, eg *vivir* (to live)

yo	viv**o**	nosotros/as	viv**imos**
tú	viv**es**	vosotros/as	viv**ís**
usted } él, ella }	viv**e**	ustedes } ellos/as }	viv**en**

B   Some verbs don't just change their endings – they have a slight, predictable change in the middle of some of their forms as well, eg:

	querer (to want)	jugar (to play)
yo	quiero	juego
tú	quieres	juegas
usted; él, ella	quiere	juega
nosotros/as	queremos	jugamos
vosotros/as	queréis	jugáis
ustedes; ellos/as	quieren	juegan

These verbs are known as radical-changing verbs and are shown as querer (ie), jugar (ue) in the Vocabulary at the back of the book.

C IRREGULAR VERBS

ser (to be)
soy	eres	es	somos	sois	son

estar (to be)
estoy	estás	está	estamos	estáis	están

ir (to go)
voy	vas	va	vamos	vais	van

dar (to give)
doy	das	da	damos	dais	dan

decir (to say)
digo	dices	dice	decimos	decís	dicen

hacer (to do)
hago	haces	hace	hacemos	hacéis	hacen

tener (to have)
tengo	tienes	tiene	tenemos	tenéis	tienen

venir (to come)
vengo	vienes	viene	venimos	venís	vienen

The present tense

Strictly speaking, there are two present tenses. The most common one is the Simple Present:

trabajo de nueve a siete	**I work** from nine to seven
ahora **trabajo** en Madrid	**I'm working** in Madrid now

So this can mean 'I work' or 'I'm working', depending on the sentence.

The other present tense is the Present Continuous, which is used to stress what someone is actually doing at the moment. It's made up of two parts: the correct form of estar (to be), plus the -ndo part (the present participle) of the main verb – this second part doesn't change:

estoy trabajando con mi cuñado	**I'm working** with my brother-in-law
¿**estás aprendiendo** español?	**are you learning** Spanish?

The past tense

This describes something that someone **did** some time ago:

el año pasado **fuimos** a Cantabria	last year **we went** to Cantabria
¿cuánto tiempo **estuviste** allí?	how long **were you** there?

The future

One of the ways of talking about the future – the equivalent to the English 'I **will** do' – is not covered. But you can get on quite well by using the equivalent of 'I'm going to . . .':

el año que viene **vamos a visitar** Gran Bretaña	next year we're going to visit Britain

This construction consists of the correct form of ir (to go), plus a, plus the infinitive of the verb describing the action.

You can also say what you're thinking of doing, using pensar plus an infinitive:

pienso ir a Mallorca	I'm thinking of going to Majorca, I intend to go to Majorca

Negatives

A straight no in front of the verb is all that's required to make a positive statement negative:

tengo hermanos	**no** tengo hermanos
mi marido está aquí	mi marido **no** está aquí

ADVERBS

Adverbs describe a verb or an adjective, eg 'slowly', 'sadly', 'quickly'. In English many adverbs end in '-ly'. In Spanish a lot of them end in -mente:

normalmente ceno a las ocho	I normally have supper at eight
probablemente	probably

Some common adverbs don't end in -mente:

bien	well	demasiado	too
mal	badly	más	more

muy	very	*menos*	less
bastante	quite, fairly		

PREPOSITIONS

Prepositions are words like 'near', 'along', 'after', which link with nouns to show where or when an action takes place. These are some examples of the more important ones, in two categories:

Place

en *la costa*	on the coast
en *el restaurante*	in the restaurant
delante de *la catedral*	in front of the cathedral
detrás de *la iglesia*	behind the church
cerca de *la plaza*	near/close to the square
lejos de *la playa*	far from the beach
por *la calle*	along the street

Time

después de *la comida*	after the meal
antes de *la cena*	before supper
a *mediodía*	at midday
sobre *las cinco*	at about five o'clock
por *la mañana*	in the morning

Grammar Summary

MEXICO VIVO

OBJECT PRONOUNS

In Spanish, the object pronouns are:

me	me, to me
te	you, to you (informal, singular)
le	you, to you (formal, singular); him, to him; her, to her
la	you (feminine, formal, singular); her; it (feminine)
lo	you (masculine, formal, singular); him; it (masculine)
nos	us, to us
os	you, to you (informal, plural)
les	you, to you (formal, plural); them, to them
las	them (feminine)
los	them (masculine)

Notice the position of object pronouns, which usually come **before** the verb in Spanish:

¿me lleva?	will you take **me**?
lo compro	I'll buy **it**

In phrases like *¿me puede ayudar?*, the pronoun can either come before the first (modal) verb or after, and attached to, the second verb (in the infinitive):
¿puede ayudarme?
Another example:
lo quiero comprar or *quiero comprarlo*

There are two differences between Mexican and peninsular Spanish usage:
1 The *os* form is not used in Mexico because the *vosotros* form of address is not used; *ustedes* refers to 'you', both 'familiar' and 'formal', in the plural.
2 In some parts of Spain *le* is used to mean 'him, her' as well as 'to him, to her' and *les* is used to mean 'them' as well as 'to them' when referring to people; *lo, la, los, las* are only used when referring to objects.
Compare the Mexican and Spanish ways of saying 'I'm seeing him tomorrow':

lo veo mañana (Mexico)
le veo mañana (Spain)

'EMPHATIC' PRONOUNS

'Emphatic' pronouns are those that follow a preposition – *a, para, por, de* etc. They are the same as the subject pronouns except in the first and second person singular:

a mí	*a nosotros*
a ti	*a vosotros* (not Mex)
a usted	*a ustedes*
a él	*a ellos*
a ella	*a ellas*

With *con*, a different form is used in the singular:
conmigo
contigo

'PERSONAL' A

When a person is the object of a verb, it must be preceded by *a*:

*veo **a** Juan*	I see Juan
*conozco **a** ellos*	I know them
*acompaño **al** director*	I'm going with the director

REFLEXIVE PRONOUNS

The reflexive pronouns (see page 36) are:

yo	**me**	llamo
tú	**te**	llamas
usted/él/ella	**se**	llama
nosotros	**nos**	llamamos
vosotros	**vos**	llamáis (not Mex)
ustedes/ellos/ellas	**se**	llaman

When the verb is in the infinitive, the reflexive pronoun usually joins on to it:
quiero bañarme
tenemos que levantarnos temprano

In the imperative, the pronoun joins on to the end of the verb:

¡siéntense!	sit down
¡abróchense los cinturones de seguridad!	fasten your seat belts

But if it is a negative command, the pronoun precedes the verb:

¡no se preocupe!	don't worry
¡no se moleste!	don't go to any trouble

Se

The pronoun se also has uses other than the reflexive:

1 with the impersonal sense of 'one' – we would tend to say 'I', 'you', 'we' or 'they' in English, depending on the context:

¿se puede estacionar aquí?	can I/we/you park here?
¿cómo se llega al centro?	how do I/we/you get to the centre?
se come muy tarde aquí	we/you/they eat very late here

2 in a passive sense:

se habla español	Spanish (is) spoken
se venden boletos	tickets (are) sold

Ser and estar

The verb ser tells you:
1 who somebody is
   Pablo es mi hermano
2 what their job is
   ella es profesora
3 what their nationality is
   Alfonso es mexicano
4 what they are like physically
   es alta
5 what sort of person they are
   es alegre

The verb estar tells you:
1 where someone/something is
   el hotel está en la colonia Florida
2 how someone is feeling
   está triste
3 what condition something is in
   está roto

IRREGULAR VERBS

conocer (to know)
conozco conoces conoce
conocemos conocéis conocen

poder (to be able to, can)
puedo puedes puede
podemos podéis pueden

poner (to put)
pongo pones pone
ponemos ponéis ponen

saber (to know)
sé sabes sabe
sabemos sabéis saben

traer (to bring)
traigo traes trae
traemos traéis traen

THE IMPERATIVE

The imperative form of the verb is used to give instructions:

pase a la caja	go to the cash desk
tome la primera a la derecha	take the first on the right

When talking to someone you would address as usted, the imperative is formed by taking the first person singular of the verb, removing the 'o' ending and replacing it as follows:
-e in the case of -ar verbs: hable, tome
-a in the case of -er and -ir verbs: viva, siga

For the ustedes form, simply add 'n' to the usted form: hablen, tomen, sigan.

These rules apply to most irregular verbs:
siga(n), venga(n), tenga(n), diga(n), ponga(n)
But there are exceptions:

vaya	(ir)
dé	(dar)
sepa	(saber)

NEGATIVES

1 If the words for 'nothing', 'nobody' or 'never' follow the verb, the verb is preceded by no:

no hace nada	he's not doing anything

no conozco a nadie	I don't know anyone
no canta nunca	he never sings

2 *Tampoco*, the negative of *también*, is used in the same way:

no me gusta tampoco la música pop	I don't like pop music either

Tampoco can also be used to agree with a negative statement:

– *No me gustan los mariachis*	I don't like mariachis
– *A mí tampoco*	Nor do I

'neither ... nor' is *ni ... ni*:

ni Pablo ni Alfonso pueden venir	neither Pablo nor Alfonso can come
no me gusta ni la carne ni el pescado	I don't like meat or fish

3 *Pero* means 'but'; however, if you are making a negative statement where two objects, actions or ideas are contrasted, *sino* replaces *pero*:
   no fui a Huatulco sino a Puerto Angel   I didn't go to Huatulco but to Puerto Angel

4 The negative of *algún* ('some') is *ningún*:

no queda ningún asiento	there aren't any seats left

no hay ninguna parada por aquí	there aren't any stops near here

COMPARATIVES

When making comparisons, put *más* or *menos* before the adjective and *que* after it:
es más bonito que Acapulco   it's prettier than Acapulco
es menos interesante que la otra película   it's less interesting than the other film
Note that some adjectives in Spanish contain the idea of comparison, so don't need *más* or *menos* in front of them: *mayor* older,   *mejor* better,   *peor* worse
Patricia es mayor que yo   Patricia is older than me
el clima es peor que en Inglaterra   the climate is worse than in England

SUPERLATIVES

To say 'biggest', 'tallest' etc:

la ciudad más grande	the biggest city
la persona más alta	the tallest person
la novela más interesante	the most interesting novel

Spanish in Mexico and Spain

THE DIFFERENCES

Many foreigners say they find it easier to understand the spoken Spanish of Mexico than that of Spain. The consonants are clearer; it is generally spoken more slowly and softly and with a more musical intonation.

PRONUNCIATION

In common with southern Spain and all Latin American countries, the *seseo* prevails in Mexico. Whereas in northern and central Spain, the letter *'c'* before an *'e'* or *'i'* and the letter *'z'* are pronounced like the *'th'* in 'thin', in Mexico they are pronounced as *'s'*. So *casa* and *caza* sound the same, as do *coser* and *cocer*.

The *'s'* sound is pronounced more forcefully than in Spain.

'J' is pronounced rather like the English 'h' in 'hand', whereas in Spain it is pronounced like the 'ch' of Scottish 'loch'.

'X' can be pronounced in a number of ways:
as *'s'*: Xochimilco
as *'h'*: Oaxaca
as *'ks'*: Necaxa
as *'sh'*: Ixtapa
It's best to learn each word as you meet it.

Mexicans are *'yeistas'*, i.e. the *'ll'* is pronounced as the 'y' of 'yes' – unlike in certain areas of Spain where it is pronounced more like the 'lli' of 'million'.

GRAMMAR

The most obvious differences are:
1   The *vosotros* form is not used: the *ustedes* form is used as the plural of *tú*.
2   The diminutive is used much more frequently in Mexico (see page 33).
3   The use of the reflexive is more common in Mexico, where in Spain the same word is used in the same context without a reflexive:
¡súbase! (Mex)   *¡suba!* (Sp) get in
¡bájese! (Mex)   *¡baje!* (Sp) get out
4   Idiomatic expressions peculiar to Mexico:
se me hace que   I think that
se me antoja salir   I feel like going out
se me descompuso el   my car broke down
   coche
5   Some other 'mexicanisms' are:
a the use of *mero* meaning *mismo* as in:
   ya mero   right now
   en la mera esquina   right on the corner
b the use of *no más* to give emphasis:
   ¡siéntese no más! do sit down
c *muy seguido* meaning 'often'
d the use of *hasta* to mean 'not until':
   me regreso a México hasta octubre I'm not going back to Mexico until October
   (In Spain this would be: *no voy a regresar a México hasta octubre*)
e *ni modo* meaning 'it can't be helped'

VOCABULARY

United States' influence accounts for differences in some words between Mexico and Spain, though this is no more prevalent than in some other Latin American countries. It is particularly obvious in sporting terms, clothing, domestic appliances and certain other aspects of modern life: *refrigerador, elevador, clutch, clóset, rentar, checar.*

Here is a list of all key words taught in **México Vivo** which are different from those used in Spain:

Mexico	Spain	
Mexico	**Spain**	
Chapter 1		
el camión	el autobús	*bus*
el sitio	la parada de taxis	*taxi-rank*
el boleto	el billete	*ticket (travel)*
	la entrada	*ticket (performance)*
la cuadra	la manzana	*block*
la colonia	el barrio	*district*
Chapter 2		
el baño	los servicios/ el lavabo	*toilet*
la central camionera	la estación/ terminal de autobuses	*coach station*
la forma	el impreso	*form*
la reservación	la reserva	*reservation*
la alberca	la piscina	*swimming pool*
el elevador	el ascensor	*lift*
la regadera	la ducha	*shower*
Chapter 3		
platicar	charlar	*to chat*
el platillo	el plato	*dish*
Chapter 5		
la licencia	el carnet/permiso de conducir	*driving licence*
la recámara	el dormitorio	*bedroom*
rentar	alquilar	*to rent*

Further reading

The following is just a selection of the many books on Mexico written in English or available in translation from the Spanish.

GUIDE BOOKS

For an overview, the *Insight Guide to Mexico* (edited by Sanford Zalburg and published by APA Productions) offers a beautifully presented panorama of the history, places and people. For practical information and a little beginners' level language, *In Mexico*, by Tim Connell and Antony Keble (EMC), is a useful and accessible introduction. For comprehensive guides, *Mexico: A Travel Survival Kit* (Lonely Planet), Fodor's *Mexico* and *Rough Guide to Mexico* (RKP) are widely available. If you want a compact 'travelling companion', the *Michelin* guide is detailed and practical; other useful guides are *The American Express Pocket Guide* (Mitchell Beazley), *Welcome to Mexico* (Collins), and Hildebrand's *Travel Guide*.

TRAVEL BOOKS

Many personal accounts of travels in Mexico have been written by foreign visitors. The 'classic' work is *Life in Mexico* (first published in 1913), the nineteenth-century memoirs of Fanny Calderón de la Barca, a Scotswoman married to the Spanish Ambassador to Mexico. It is interesting to compare *Viva México!* by Charles Macomb Flandrow (Eland Books), whimsical observations of life in Mexico, and *Barbarous Mexico* (University of Texas Press) by John Kenneth Turner, who exposed the terrible conditions prevailing on the henequen plantations during the dictatorship of Porfirio Díaz. Another interesting comparison is between *Mornings in Mexico* by D. H. Lawrence (Penguin) and *The Lawless Roads* by Graham Greene (Penguin) – the latter a very sombre picture of his travels in the 1930s.

SOCIETY

The work of the social anthropologist Oscar Lewis offers much insight into the lives of a poor working-class family in Mexico City in the 40s and 50s: *The Children of Sánchez* and *A Death in the Sánchez Family* (both published by Penguin); and his study of a Zapatista peasant *Pedro Martínez* describes aspects of rural life and the Revolution. The 'jungle novels' of Ben Traven (pub. Allison and Busby) also examine working conditions and society in pre-revolutionary Mexico. Gregory Reck's *In the Shadow of Tlaloc* (Penguin) presents a more contemporary view of life in a Mexican village. For a thought-provoking view of contemporary life and politics, Alan Riding, a former *New York Times* correspondent to Mexico, offers a fascinating account in *Mexico: Inside the Volcano* (Coronet Books).

ANCIENT CIVILIZATIONS

As a 'starter' for the indigenous cultures, *Of Gods and Men* (BBC Books), based on the television series, is a fascinating study of the pre-Hispanic civilizations and the way in which their customs and beliefs have survived today. On more specific topics, *Mexico: Ancient Peoples and Places* (Oklahoma Press) and *The Maya* (Penguin) both by Michael D. Coe, *Maya History and Religion* (Oklahoma Press) by Eric J. Thompson and, for a very recent study, *The Blood of Kings* (Sotheby's) by Linda Schele and Mary-Ellen Miller; *The Aztecs, People of the Sun* (Oklahoma Press) by Alfonso Caso; Jacques Soustelle's *Daily Life of the Aztecs* (André Deutsch) and Nigel Davies' *The Ancient Kingdoms of Mexico* (Penguin).

HISTORY AND THE REVOLUTION

For an eye-witness account of the conquest of Mexico, read the epic *The Conquest of New Spain* (Penguin) by Bernal Díaz who accompanied Cortés throughout his campaign. It conveys the Spaniards' amazement as they contemplated La Gran Tenochtitlán for the first time. Based on this account is the classic nineteenth-century history by William Prescott *History of the Conquest of Mexico* – a voluminous tome which can be 'dipped into'. A graphic anecdotal account of the Mexican Revolution – fascinating for its portrait of Pancho Villa – is John Reed's *Insurgent Mexico* (New World). For studies of Emiliano Zapata, John Womack's in-depth analysis *Zapata and the Mexican Revolution* (Penguin); *The Wind that Swept Mexico* (University of Texas) by Anita Brenner and George Leighton, is brief but has very interesting photographs. For a comprehensive study of Mexican history, *The Course of Mexican History* by Michael Meyer and William Sherman is a good start. There are many more!

ART

There are two excellent catalogues on the work of Rivera and Orozco: for Rivera, the one published by the Detroit Institute of Arts for the exhibition in 1986, and for Orozco, that of the Museum of Modern Art, Oxford, 1980. Desmond Rochfort's *The Murals of Diego Rivera* (South Bank) is a very useful guide, and Hayden Herrera's biography of Frida Kahlo, *Frida, a Biography*, gives many fascinating details of her life.

POETRY

The temples of the Indian peoples were destroyed but their culture survived because Spanish priests learned Indian languages to facilitate the task of conversion. Fray Bernadino de Sahagún (1500–70) collected copious material in Nahuatl and wrote volumes of information on *'las cosas de la Nueva España'* (as Mexico was called in colonial times). These writings show the importance of lyrical poetry, which was considered a 'noble art' in pre-Hispanic society. The verses of the poet-king Netzahualcoyotl, for example, are as moving today as when they were written hundreds of years ago. The 'noble art' has continued and flourished in Mexico, particularly in the twentieth century with poets such as Ramón

López Velarde, José Gorostiza, Salvador Novo, Carlos Pellicer, Jaime Sabines and José Emilio Pacheco, to mention only a few. Mexico's greatest living poet, Octavio Paz, has received international acclaim. His poem *Piedra de Sol* (Sunstone) has the same number of lines as there were days in the Aztec year.

THE NOVEL

The novel in Mexico began to flourish during and after the Revolution of 1910: Mariano Azuela is the pioneer with his portrayal of Mexican society at that time. In the work of Martín Luis Guzmán the personalities and the power-struggles of the leaders emerge, and Gregorio López y Fuentes reveals, for the first time, the way of life of the Indians. Juan Rulfo's *Pedro Páramo* (1955) is recognised as one of the greatest works in contemporary Latin American writing. It portrays a rural Mexico which the Revolution swept away, but whose essence remains. Carlos Fuentes, whose works are more widely-known than those of any other Mexican author, reveals the society which emerged after the Revolution, and reflects on a vast range of historical, political, social and literary themes. Two writers who chronicle contemporary events and evaluate Mexican society with great perception and humanity are Carlos Monsivais and Elena Poniatowska.

LANGUAGE

Finally, if you wish to broaden your linguistic horizons and look at Spanish in other Latin American countries, a practical introduction is given in the supplement to the *Ealing Spanish Course, Introduction to Latin America* (Longman). *Paso Doble* (BBC Books) also features language from various Latin American countries. A classic work on the Spanish in Spain and Latin America is *The Spanish Language* by W. J. Entwistle. A very detailed study is provided in *Spanish in the Americas* (Georgetown University) by Eleanor Greet Cotten and John M. Sharp. In Spanish, *Perspectivas Culturales de Hispanoamérica* (National Textbook Company) by Juan Kattán-Ibarra gives a full introduction to all aspects of Latin American society and can be used as a more advanced language work book.

Key

CHAPTER 1

Spot-check

1 1 Because he's got luggage
   2 As you go out, on your right
2 1 In the Cuauhtémoc district
   2 10,500 pesos
3 At the corner, by the traffic lights
4 1 He should turn right
   2 About 20 minutes

¿Verdad?

A 1 false   2 true
B 1 false   2 true
C 1 false   2 true

Can you . . .?

a ¿Me puede ayudar con mi equipaje?
b ¿Me puede decir cómo se llama esta calle?
c ¿Me puede llevar al Museo de Antropología?
d ¿Me puede esperar en la esquina de Londres con Florencia?
e ¿Me puede dejar enfrente del cine?
f ¿Me puede decir dónde puedo tomar un camión a la Alameda?

Crossed lines

1b, 2d, 3f, 4a, 5c, 6e

Over to you

You: Disculpe/Discúlpeme. ¿Cómo llego/voy al Museo de Arte Moderno?
You: ¿Está muy lejos?
You: Está bien. Puedo ir a pie.
You: ¿Está a mano derecha o izquierda?
You: Muchas gracias.

Lost!

a Saliendo del hotel sigue hasta el semáforo y da vuelta a la izquierda.
b Por favor, ¿me puede decir cómo llego a la Avenida Juárez?
c ¿Hay una estación de metro por aquí?
d Siga todo derecho hasta llegar a la Avenida Juárez.
e El banco está detrás de la Alameda.
f Hay un sitio de taxis a dos cuadras de aquí, a mano izquierda.

Missing link

a te b nos c las d lo e me f los
g los h nos

Say it in Spanish

a No puedo ver a Juan hoy.
b ¿Y a usted, le gusta México?
c No pueden llevar a Angeles al aeropuerto.
d A mí, me gusta la comida mexicana. ¿Y a ti?
e Podemos esperar a Susanita en el bar.
f A Mauricio le gustan las ciudades grandes pero a mí no.

Odd one out

a hola b automático c maleta d camión
e esperar f ahora g ayudar

Sopa de Letras

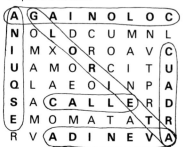

¿Conoce usted México?

a false b false c true d false
e false f false g true h false

CHAPTER 2

Spot-check

1 1 7 hours and 10 minutes
   2 No
2 1 No
   2 Gate 46
3 1 For three nights
   2 No
4 1 2,530 pesos
   2 As proof of identity

¿Verdad?

A 1 true   2 false
B 1 false   2 false
C 1 false   2 false
D 1 true   2 false

Say it in Spanish

a Tengo que cambiar unos cheques de viajero.
b ¿Cuánto dura el vuelo a Villahermosa?
c Santiago y Patricia tienen que ir a la central de autobuses.
d ¿A cómo está el dólar?
e ¿Qué día es hoy?
f ¿Puedo pagar con tarjeta de crédito?
g Juan no puede trabajar los sábados.
h ¿Qué haces los fines de semana?

The other half

1 f, 2 d, 3 e, 4 a, 5 c, 6 b

Over to you

You: Buenas tardes. Quiero ir a Acapulco mañana en la mañana, si es posible.
You: Está bien. ¿A qué hora es el vuelo?
You: Prefiero el vuelo de la mañana.
You: ¡Cómo no! . . . y aquí tiene mi tarjeta de crédito.

Answer back

1 b, 2 e, 3 d, 4 c, 5 a, 6 f

Order please

a Llame al sitio, por favor.
b Cierre la puerta, por favor.
c Firme aquí, por favor.
d Espere un momento, por favor.
e Déjeme en la esquina, por favor.

a ¿Puede llamar al sitio, por favor?
b ¿Puede cerrar la puerta, por favor?
c ¿Puede firmar aquí, por favor?
d ¿Puede esperar un momento, por favor?
e ¿Puede dejarme en la esquina, por favor?

Missing link

a Se b Te c se d nos e se f Me g se

In the right order

e, d, f, a, c, b

Over to you

You: Buenas tardes. Quiero dos boletos para la Ciudad de México.
You: Para la salida de las 11 esta noche.
You: ¿Hay dos asientos en el medio?
You: ¿Hay alguno delante?
You: Preferimos estar juntos. Dénos dos detrás, por favor.

A question of time

a dura b dura c tardar d tarda e tardo

Excuses, excuses

a No puedo ayudar. Tengo que ir al aeropuerto.
b Tú no puedes ir. Tienes que trabajar esta noche.
c No podemos esperar. Tenemos que tomar un vuelo a Acapulco.
d No pueden venir. Tienen que ver a un amigo esta noche.
e No puede hablar ahora. Tiene que venir mañana.

Hotel rules

a yes b to reception c 15% d have a shower
e twelve o'clock f no

Crucigrama

1 regadera 2 alberca 3 fecha 4 reservación
5 asiento 6 tardar 7 forma 8 durar
Secret word = elevador

¿Conoce usted México?

a false b true c false d false
e true f true g true h false

CHAPTER 3

Spot-check

1 1 Today
    2 At two o'clock
2 1 The 0
    2 Because he's not in the office
3 1 Because of the heavy traffic
    2 Yes

¿Verdad?

A 1 false 2 false
B 1 false 2 false
C 1 false 2 true
D 1 false 2 true

Gaps

a se pronuncia, b se abre, c se sirve,
d se habla, e se aceptan, f se dice,
g se hablan, h se venden

Matches

a 4, b 5, c 2, d 7, e 8, f 1, g 6, h 3

Over to you

You: Buenos días. ¿Se encuentra Leticia?/¿Está
    Leticia?

You: ¿ A qué hora podría llamarla?
You: No puedo llamar esta noche. ¿Podría dejar un
    recado?
You: De . . . Lo siento mucho, pero no puedo verla
    mañana. Tengo que ir a Toluca.
You: Muy amable. Hasta luego.

¡No me digas!

a ¡qué horror!
b ¡felicidades!
c ¡qué lindo eres!
d ¡qué bonito!
e ¡qué lástima!
f ¡qué bien!

Pairs

a 3, b 7, c 9, d 8, e 1, f 2, g 4,
h 5, i 6

¡Capitán!

a el ceviche acapulqueño
b la sopa de verduras mixtas
c los ostiones empanizados con salsa tártara
d el filete de pescado a la parrilla
e el cóctel de aguacate
f el filete de res con salsa mostaza
g los tacos de cochinita pibil
h el filete de pescado al mojo de ajo
i las enchiladas con frijoles

La línea está malísima

1 encuentra
2 va
3 dejar/recado
4 Del
5 preguntarle/posible
6 bien/Hasta

Answer back

a 4, b 9, c 8, d 5, e 6, f 7, g 3,
h 1, i 2

Odd one out

a mantequilla b papa c mole d sandía
e hamburguesa f encontrar g llevar

Out of order

h, c, i, f, b, a, d, g, e

Crossed lines

g 8, a 2, f 1, b 4, e 3, c 5, d 6, h 7

¿Conoce usted México?

a false b true c false d false e true
f false g false h false i false

CHAPTER 4

Spot-check

1 Two people
2 None
3 Three
4 One

¿Verdad?

A 1 false   2 false
B false
C 1 false   2 false

Say it in Spanish

a Supongo que sí.
b No estoy de acuerdo.
c Tienes razón.
d Depende del tiempo.
e No tiene ganas de ir.
f ¿Qué piensas/opinas de la película?/¿Qué te parece la película?
g Nunca como hamburguesas/No como nunca hamburguesas.
h No conozco a nadie.
i Este restaurante es mejor que el otro.

Blanco y Negro

guapo-feo
nunca-siempre
alto-bajo
todos-nadie
también-tampoco
subir-bajar
delante-detrás
algún-ningún
libre-ocupado
aburrido-divertido

Gaps

a pero b pero c sino d también
e tampoco f también g tampoco h ni/ni

Over to you

You: Sí, le/lo conozco bastante bien.
You: Es muy agradable y muy inteligente.
You: Sí, tiene veinticuatro años.
You: No, se parece a su padre, y es mucho más alto que Jorge.
You: Sí, creo que es muy simpático.

Do you know?

a sabe, b conocemos, c sabes, d saber,
e conozco/sé, f conocer, g sabes, h conoces

Answer back

1 e, 2 c, 3 f, 4 b, 5 a, 6 d

Cóctel de letras

a simpático, b ninguna, c opinar,
d aburrido, e guapo, f nadie

A matter of opinion

a parecen, b prefieres, c gusta, d creo,
e parece, f prefiero, g parece, h opina(s)
i pareces, j gusta/prefiero

La vida es cruel

Nadie/Algunas/algún/ninguna/ninguna/alguien

About people

1 c, 2 c, 3 b, 4 b, 5 c, 6 b

¿Conoce usted México?

a false b true c false d false
e true f false g false

CHAPTER 5

Spot-check

1 1 No
2 At Mérida airport
2 1 No
2 The day after tomorrow
3 1 Dive on the reef
2 Information about the excursions to the coast
4 1 50,000 pesos
2 One day

¿Verdad?

A 1 false 2 true
B 1 false 2 true
C 1 false 2 false

Say it in Spanish

a Me gustaría ir a Mérida.
b ¿Cuándo puedo recoger el coche?
c ¿Cuánto cuesta por día?
d Necesito { una batería nueva.
una pila nueva.
e ¿Me podría recomendar un buen restaurante?
f ¿Cuándo vuelves a Londres?
g ¿Es posible cambiar mi boleto?
h Me gustaría desayunar en mi habitación.
i ¿Cuánto tiempo va a tardar en repararlo/arreglarlo?

¿Por o para?

a Para/por b por c para d Para e por
f para g para h por i para j por

On the road

You: Buenas tardes. Me gustaría rentar un coche pequeño.
You: Para hoy, si es posible.
You: Para cinco días, hasta el sábado.
You: Gracias. Quiero saber si podría dejarlo en el aeropuerto de Mérida o ¿tengo que devolverlo aquí?
You: ¿Están los seguros incluidos en el precio?
You: Los coches pequeños no tienen aire acondicionado, ¿verdad?
You: Entonces, me gustaría rentar un coche más grande, pero no demasiado caro.

Help

a la relojería b la óptica c la zapatería
d el taller mecánico e la lavandería

Se compra, se vende

1 e, 2 c, 3 d, 4 b, 5 a

No hay problema

You: Hola. Mi regadera no funciona. ¿Es posible repararla esta tarde?
You: (Bueno), entonces, me gustaría cambiar de habitación.
You: Muchas gracias. También tengo (alguna) ropa para lavar. ¿Hay (una) lavandería aquí?
You: ¿Sabe usted cuándo estará/va a estar lista la ropa?
You: Pero la necesito para esta noche.

Car hire

a 43 b 7.9.1992 c Colonia Roma
d 11590 D.F. e director f 3
g yes h 25 April 1990

¿Conoce usted México?

a true b false c false d true
e false f true g false

Translation of *Lecturas*

As these translations are intended to be a reference to check the meaning of a word or phrase, the translation is as close as possible to the Spanish and not necessarily in the best style of English.

CHAPTER 1

Mexico City, yesterday and today

At two thousand metres, Mexico City is surrounded by mountains and volcanoes.

Its site was chosen by the Aztecs, who founded the city in 1325, naming it Tenochtitlán. It was the capital of their empire until the Spanish conquest in 1521.

The Spanish destroyed the Aztec Empire. On the ruins of Tenochtitlán, they built a new city.

Today, traces of the Aztec and Spanish past of this great capital can still be seen. It is the most heavily-populated city in the world, with 19 million inhabitants. It is an industrial city where a quarter of the country's population lives. For its inhabitants, pollution and traffic are two of the capital's most serious problems. But in spite of the problems, the people of Mexico City feel a great affection for their city.

The city of miracles

Many of the millions of inhabitants of Mexico City are 'emigrants' who abandoned the countryside for the capital. One of these is Cristina Pacheco, a popular journalist and writer.

For Cristina, the longest street in the world, la Avenida de los Insurgentes, is a good example of the city's complexity.

In the north, the road goes as far as the poor district of Indios Verdes, where thousands of immigrants live, people who came here in the hope of finding a better life. As Cristina says, 'they come in search of a dream, a fantasy, a possibility'.

Indios Verdes shows one of the faces of the city. But twenty kilometres south, Insurgentes goes through a very different area: the prosperous centre. This was a part of the city badly affected by the earthquake of 1985, always present in the memory of Mexicans. 'It's terrible to see the city where you grew up, where you have everything you love most, suddenly falling to pieces.'

Further south on Insurgentes are peaceful and exclusive residential districts where poverty does not exist.

Certainly a city of contrasts, Cristina defines Mexico City as 'a city of miracles', affirming that 'the most populous city in the world is also the most generous'.

CHAPTER 2

The rugs of Teotitlán

For the Indians of Oaxaca, craftwork has traditionally been a way of supplementing meagre earnings: the state is one of the poorest in Mexico.

Recently, however, there has been a revaluation of craftwork. Because of commercial pressures, some craftspeople have adopted modern, industrial techniques, abandoning the more traditional ones.

But craftspeople like the Mendoza family, Zapotec Indians, have retained the methods of their forefathers. They make rugs – a flourishing business in the village of Teotitlán.

In the Mendoza house, all the wool is spun and dyed by hand. To colour it, natural local products are utilised, such as 'rock moss' and cochineal. In the design of the carpets they use Zapotec motifs from before the Spanish conquest. Although Emiliano, the father, has also done commissions for abstract art, he says he prefers the old designs. 'It's a tradition of the Zapotec race . . . And I like the fact that we're not losing traditional things.'

The Mendozas are a good example of how modern life, in some respects, can help maintain the identity of Indian groups.

Doctors and healers

In many communities in Oaxaca, as in the town of Tlaxiaco, native medicine is still alive.

The stalls of medicinal plants which sell remedies for almost all ills are typical of any market. And the traditional Indian doctors, 'healers', continue to practise their healing arts.

Angélica Hernández has been a healer in Tlaxiaco since she was very young. As well as using plants, Angélica recognises the importance of the Catholic religion in the healing process: 'The most important factor is faith'.

However, modern medicine also exists in the town. There is a state-run hospital and Dr. Javier Bautista gives classes in health education in the schools. Javier thinks that, 'The modern doctor forgets about many things which the Indian doctor sees – like the family, the environment in which people live'.

The doctor thinks that a balance between modern and Indian medicine is necessary to ensure the well-being and the future of Mexican Indians.

CHAPTER 3

Land and liberty

Since it began to be cultivated in Mesoamerica, maize has constituted the basic element of the Mexican diet, occupying a central place in religions, legends and customs.

Today, as in the past, the *tortilla* is the most typical product made from maize. It can be eaten on its own, and it is also the basis of some 150 different dishes.

At present, maize represents a very important part of agricultural production in Mexico – a country where only 15% of the soil is arable. Traditionally, this fertile land was the property of a few rich landowners. Fair distribution of the land was the main objective of the 1910 Revolution, one of whose leaders was the great Emiliano Zapata. Today, in Morelos, his son Mateo continues working the land, and remembers his father in these words: 'For the people, he represents a liberator: for me, as his son, he represents the very best as a father'.

Emiliano Zapata, one of the most charismatic heroes in Mexican history, was assassinated in 1919. Post-revolutionary governments have distributed more than half of the arable land, but agricultural reform has not yet finished. As Saúl Ríos, from the Ministry of Agricultural Reform, explains: 'The self-sufficiency of our country in food remains to be achieved'.

Black gold

Oil is the motor of the Mexican economy. It is the country's main export and gives work to over a million people.

In the state of Tabasco is the city of Reforma, where new deposits of oil were found at the beginning of the 70s. The arrival of Pemex, the state-run oil company, totally changed the appearance of the community. Clinics, schools and an industrial estate were built, as well as the first road into the town.

Near Reforma is one of the biggest petrochemical plants in the country – Cactus. The plant has as neighbours the Ruiz brothers, ranch owners who are involved in the traditional activity of Tabasco: cattle. The closeness of the ranch to Cactus causes certain problems, the most serious of which is pollution. The plant produces a lot of acid gases and as Guillermo Ruiz says: 'The wire fencing is destroyed in six months . . . there's a constant drizzle of oil here in the ranch.'

Researchers at Pemex regularly monitor the level of pollution, and the Ruiz brothers are not pessimistic about the future. 'I think it's a good thing, what we have now. I wouldn't like to go back to the past,' says Mariano Ruiz.

But perhaps the presence of Pemex will not be so welcome in the future if the problem of pollution is not solved.

CHAPTER 4

A dance class

Gloria Contreras is the most important figure in contemporary dance in Mexico. Dance has a long tradition in the country, but courses of contemporary dance like those directed by Gloria in the Autonomous University are unusual.

At present, Gloria has more than 300 pupils and, with one exception, none of them is professional. In spite of their other activities, they spend long hours perfecting their techniques. For Susan Schinkel, one of the students, 'Dancing is a moment of absorption . . . of tranquillity through which you get rid of all your tensions'.

Another of the students is Roberto Quintana, the only man in the class. Being male, he has had to overcome many prejudices in order to devote himself to dance: 'Mexican families don't let their children, especially the males, get involved in these kind of activities.'

At the moment, the group is rehearsing a Mexican dance, 'Sensemayá', by the composer Silvestre Revueltas. It is an evocation of Mexico's hispanic past.

Despite the success of the classes, their future is uncertain because of the economic crisis the country is undergoing. But Gloria is not pessimistic: 'I hope that, in spite of the crisis, we can continue performing and proving that Mexican dance has a place in the world.'

Carlos Fuentes on Mexican culture

Carlos Fuentes is one of the best known writers and intellectuals in Mexico today. Among his most important works are *Where the Air is Clear* and *The Death of Artemio Cruz*. We asked him how Mexico is affected by its proximity to such a powerful country as the United States. This was his reply.

'Mexico is a country which keeps alive its Indian culture, a memory of its Indian past, a memory of its Spanish, European, medieval, Mediterranean past. It is a country which wants to go forward but without sacrificing its past. This is, for me, a fundamental truth about Mexico, it's an essential fact which characterises the country and gives it a fundamental value, above all in its frontier position . . . being a frontier with the United States – but not just the Mexican frontier but the frontier of Latin America at the same time.

Mexico and Latin America are having an increasing influence in the United States through their literature, through their music, through the political reality of our countries, through the presence of so many people of Hispano-American origin throughout the United States. And they are the bearers of very important cultural values, sometimes cultural values which have been lost in the United States.'

CHAPTER 5

The magic of the Maya

Palenque is one of the most important Mayan archaeological sites. Situated on the edge of the tropical rain-forest, it was a great city 1,300 years ago, with an area of 12 square kilometres. Today, the only part which can be seen is the centre; the rest of the city is still to be excavated.

After its decline, Palenque remained hidden until the eighteenth century, when its ruins were discovered. In 1949, the archaeologist Alberto Ruz made a spectacular discovery. After four years of excavations, he found the funeral crypt of the most important governor of Palenque, 'Shield of the Sun'. No other Maya pyramid built specially to contain a tomb has been found.

At present, the archaeologist responsible for research is Rosalba Nieto. She is now working on a map which shows all the buildings in the city. Her main concern is the conservation of the ruins. 'The forest and the constant rain are slowly destroying the buildings. Now we no longer try to excavate but rather to conserve what we have already excavated.'

For Rosalba, Palenque 'is a very, very special site. The first time I was here I felt something magic. Each day you feel something different, something you don't feel at any other site. Perhaps it's due to the grandeur of the forest, the grandeur of the Mayas.'

The coral reef

Each year, thousands of tourists come to Cancún in search of the perfect holiday. Twenty years ago, the city was just a sand-bar; today, it is an international tourist centre which continues growing at a rapid pace.

One of the big attractions for visitors is the coral reef, one of the most important in the world. Corals are sensitive organisms, very vulnerable to human presence. Biologist Eric Jordán, who is studying them, states that tourism 'directly affects the reef through physical contact, breaking things, killing fishes, taking souvenirs'.

Tourists can destroy a reef in a matter of a few years. It is for this reason that some dive masters like Alberto Friscione have decided to include an ecological message in their classes. Alberto tells his students: 'I beg you not to touch anything, not to break anything and above all, not to bring souvenirs back with you.'

Although the tourist industry exerts a continuous pressure on the delicate eco-system, the future death of the reef can still be avoided if the necessary measures are taken. According to Eric Jordán, the balance between tourism and the preservation of the coral reef is 'perfectly possible'. The reef 'can continue being a very important economic resource'.

Word groups

These word groups provide extra useful vocabulary relating to some areas covered in the book:

1 **The Spanish alphabet**
2 **Food**
3 **In the restaurant**
4 **The car**
5 **The house**
6 **Services**

1 THE SPANISH ALPHABET

Below are the letters of the Spanish alphabet and the Spanish names for them:

a	*a*	n	*ene*
b	*be*	ñ	*eñe*
c	*ce*	o	*o*
ch	*che**	p	*pe*
d	*de*	q	*cu*
e	*e*	r	*ere*
f	*efe*	s	*ese*
g	*ge*	t	*te*
h	*ache*	u	*u*
i	*i*	v	*uve*
j	*jota*	w	*doble u*
k	*ka*	x	*equis*
l	*ele*	y	*i griega*
ll	*elle*	z	*zeta*
m	*eme*		

* If spelling out a word, 'ch' is usually split into *ce* and *ache*.

2 FOOD

El desayuno	*Breakfast*
el cereal	cereal
los hot cakes (Mex)	(Scotch) pancakes
el jugo	juice
la mermelada	jam
la miel	honey or syrup
el pan dulce	sweet rolls/pastries

La fruta	*Fruit*
el durazno	peach
la lima }	lime (used instead of
el limón }	lemon)
el melón	melon
la papaya	paw-paw
la piña	pineapple
el plátano	banana
la sandía	water-melon

El pescado	*Fish*
el camarón	prawn
el ceviche	raw fish marinated in lime juice
el huachinango (Mex)	red snapper
el ostión (Mex) }	oyster
la ostra (Sp) }	

La carne	*Meat*
el cabrito	kid
la carne a la tampiqueña	slices of beef served with an *enchilada*, *guacamole* and *frijoles*
la carne de res (Mex)	beef
las carnitas (Mex)	small pieces of grilled pork
el cerdo	pork
el cordero	lamb
la cochinita pibil (Mex)	spicy pork Yucatan-style
el pavo	turkey
las puntas de filete (Mex)	thin slices of beef, often served in a sandwich
la salchicha	sausage
el tocino	bacon

Miscelánea mexicana	*Some Mexican specialities*
la botana (Mex)	appetiser
la crepa (Mex)	pancake

las enchiladas suizas (Mex)	tortilla filled with chicken, covered in a sauce, baked and topped with cheese and cream
el guacamole (Mex)	spicy purée of avocado
el huitlacoche (Mex)	edible black fungus
los nachos (Mex)	filled *totopos*
los tamales (Mex)	dumplings (can be sweet or savoury)
la torta (Mex)	a roll filled with ham/turkey etc. and avocado, lettuce, cream
los totopos (Mex)	taco shells for dips

Como se prepara	*Ways of preparing*
al horno	baked/roast
asado	roast
a la parrilla } **a la plancha** }	grilled
empanizado (Mex) } **empanado** (Sp) }	fried in breadcrumbs
gratinado	with melted cheese
al mojo de ajo (Mex)	fried in butter with garlic
pibil (Mex)	baked in banana leaves
la salsa	sauce

Legumbres y verduras	*Vegetables*
el aguacate	avocado
la alcachofa	artichoke
el arroz	rice
el apio	celery
el berro	watercress
el cacahuate (Mex) } **el cacahuete** (Sp) }	peanut
la calabaza	pumpkin
la cebolla	onion
el chile	chilli – many varieties: *habanero* is the hottest, *jalapeño* is also pungent
la espinaca	spinach
el frijol (Mex)	black bean
los frijoles refritos (Mex)	purée of black beans
el jitomate (Mex) } **el tomate** }	tomato
la lechuga	lettuce
la papa (Mex) } **la patata** (Sp) }	potato

las papas francesas (Mex)	chips, French fries
el pimiento (morrón)	pepper (capsicum)
la zanahoria	carrot

Los postres	*Desserts*
el ate (Mex)	quince jelly (often served with cheese)
las crepas con cajeta (Mex)	pancakes with a sweet sauce like condensed milk
los chongos (Mex)	junket with cinnamon
el flan	crème caramel
la gelatina	jelly
el pastel	cake
el pie (Mex)	pie
la tarta de manzana	apple tart
la manzana al horno	baked apple

Mexican desserts are usually very sweet, but if you like fruit, *mousse de mango* or *mousse de mamey* are delicious.

Las bebidas	*Drinks*
la horchata	a refreshing drink made with ground almonds or rice in Mexico (or with tiger nuts in Spain)
el licuado de agua/ leche (Mex)	freshly-squeezed fruit juices diluted with water/milk
la limonada preparada (Mex)	freshly-made lemonade
el refresco	soft drink
la sangrita (Mex)	fruit juice with tomato and tabasco sauce served in a small glass to accompany *tequila*

3 IN THE RESTAURANT

el capitán (Mex)	maître, head waiter
el/la mesero/a (Mex) } **el/la camerero/a** (Sp) }	waiter/waitress

la comida corrida (Mex) } set-price meal
el menú (Sp)

ordenar (Mex) } to order
pedir (Sp)

recomendar — to recommend
la especialidad — speciality

el platillo (Mex) } dish (of food)
el plato (Sp)

la orden (Mex) } portion
la ración (Sp)

la temporada — season

el plato — plate
los cubiertos — cutlery
el cuchillo — knife
la cuchara — spoon
la cucharita — tea-spoon
el tenedor — fork

el popote (Mex) } straw
la paja (Sp)

la servilleta — napkin
el carrito — sweet trolley

la charola (Mex) } tray
la bandeja (Sp)

el bolillo — roll
la mantequilla — butter
la pimienta — pepper
la sal — salt

4 THE CAR

el acelerador — accelerator
la bujía — spark plug

la caja de velocidades (Mex) } gear box
la caja de cambios (Sp)

la cajuela (Mex) } boot
el maletero (Sp)

el carburador — carburettor

el cofre (Mex) } bonnet
el capó (Sp)

el clutch (Mex) } clutch
el embrague (Sp)

el (tubo de) escape — exhaust (pipe)
los faros — head lights
el freno — brake

la llanta } tyre
el neumático (Sp)

el motor — engine
el parabrisas — windscreen

ponchado/a (Mex) } punctured
pinchado/a (Sp)

el radiador — radiator

las refacciones (Mex)
las piezas de
repuesto/de } spare parts
recambio (Sp)

el volante — steering wheel

In Mexico, *los Angeles Verdes* are a breakdown service provided for tourists by the government. They patrol the major highways and can carry out minor repairs.

Toll roads in Mexico are identified by the word *cuota*, the alternative route by the word *libre*.

5 THE HOUSE

el balcón — balcony
la calefacción — heating
la cama — bed

la recámara (Mex)
la alcoba/el } bedroom
dormitorio

la cerradura — lock

la clavija (Mex) } plug
el enchufe (Sp)

el clóset (Mex) } cupboard
el armario (Sp)

la cocina — kitchen

el cilindro/tanque (Mex) } gas cylinder
la bombona (Sp)

la electricidad — electricity

la estufa (Mex) } cooker
la cocina (Sp)

el foco (Mex) } bulb
la bombilla (Sp)

el fusible — fuse
el fregadero — sink

el interruptor	switch
el jardín	garden
la lámpara	lamp
el lavabo	wash-basin
la luz	light
la llave (de agua) (Mex) ⎱ **el grifo** (Sp) ⎰	tap
la mesa	table
el refrigerador (Mex) ⎱ **la nevera** (Sp) ⎰	fridge
el ropero (Mex) ⎱ **el guardarropa** (Sp) ⎰	wardrobe
la sala	lounge
la silla	chair
el suelo/el piso	floor
el techo	ceiling
la terraza	terrace
la tina (Mex) ⎱ **el baño** (Sp) ⎰	bath
la tubería	pipes
la vajilla	crockery

6 SERVICES

el albañil	builder
el carpintero	carpenter
el/la dentista	dentist
el electricista	electrician
el/la médico	doctor
el/la oftalmólogo/a	ophthalmologist
el/la oculista	oculist
el pintor	decorator
el plomero (Mex) ⎱ **el fontanero** (Sp) ⎰	plumber

Vocabulary

Notes

1. The English translations apply to words as they are used in this book.
2. Adjectives which have different endings for masculine and feminine are shown thus: *caro/a*.
3. Verbs: regular verbs follow the pattern shown on page 90. Irregular verbs: for those followed by (**i**), (**ie**) or (**ue**), see page 91; for those marked *, see pages 91 or 94.
4. Remember that **ch**, **ll** and **ñ** are separate letters in the Spanish alphabet, following **c**, **l** and **n** respectively.
5. Abbreviations: f = feminine, pl = plural, coll = colloquial.

A

abierto/a *open*
abordar: la tarjeta de abordar (*Mex*) *boarding card*
el abrazo *hug*
abrir *to open*
abrocharse *to fasten*
aburrido/a *boring*
acá *here*
acabar de *to have just*
la acción *action*
el aceite *oil*
aceptar *to accept*
acompañar *to accompany*
acostarse *to go to bed*
de acuerdo *in agreement; fine, OK*
adelantar *to move forward*
además *also*
adiós *goodbye*
el aeropuerto *airport*
agradable *agreeable, pleasant*
agradecer *to thank*
el aguacate *avocado*
ahí *there*
ahora *now*
ahorita *now, in a moment*

el aire acondicionado *air-conditioning*
el ajo *garlic*
la alberca *swimming pool* (*Mex*)
alegre *happy, cheerful*
el alemán *German*
la aleta *flipper*
alguien *someone*
algún/alguna *any; some*
alquilar *to rent*
alrededor de *around; about*
alto/a *tall, high*
allá *there*
allí *there*
amable *kind*
el/la amigo/a *friend*
la amistad *friendship*
amplio/a *spacious*
amueblado/a *furnished*
andar *go*
¡ándale! (*Mex coll.*) *OK then*
el animalito *small animal*
antes *before*
la antigüedad *antiquity*
antojarse *to fancy*
anunciar *to announce*
el año *year*
el apellido *surname*
apenas *hardly, scarcely*
el aperitivo *aperitive*
aproximadamente *approximately*
apuntar *to note*
aquel/aquella *that*
aquí *here*
arqueológico/a *archaeological*
arrancar *to start* (*of a car*)
el arrecife *reef*
arreglar *to fix*
el arroz *rice*
el arte *art*
las artesanías *craftwork*
asado/a *roast*

así *thus, in this/that way*
el asiento *seat*
atorado/a *stuck, jammed*
atrás *back, in the rear*
el auditorio *auditorium*
el auto *car*
el autobús *bus, coach*
automático/a *automatic*
la avenida *avenue*
la aventura *adventure*
las aves *poultry, birds*
el avión *plane*
el aviso *notice*
ayudar *to help*

B

el baile *dance*
la bajada *descent*
bajarse de *to get off*
bajo/a *low, short*
el balcón *balcony*
el banco *bank*
la banda *fan-belt*
la bandera *flag*
bañarse *to swim*
el baño *bath, toilet; bathroom (Mex)*
barato/a *cheap*
bastante *fairly, quite*
la batería *car battery*
Belice *Belize*
bellas artes *fine arts*
el beso *kiss*
la biblioteca *library*
bien *well, fine; right*
bienvenido/a *welcome*
el billete *ticket*
la biósfera *biosphere*
blanco/a *white*
la boda *wedding*
el bolero *bolero (dance)*
el boleto *ticket*
la bolsa *bag*
bonito/a *pretty*
bordado/a *embroidered*
la botana (*Mex*) *appetiser*
bucear *to dive*

bueno/a *good*
buscar *to look for*

C

el caballo *horse*
la cabeza *head*
el cabrito *kid*
cada *each, every*
caer *to fall*
el café *coffee*
la caja *cash-desk*
la cajuela (*Mex*) *boot (of car)*
la calabaza *pumpkin*
la calavera *skull*
calentar *to heat up*
la calidad *quality*
el calor *heat*
la calzada *roadway*
la calle *street*
la cama *bed*
la cámara *camera*
el camarón *prawn*
cambiar *to change*
caminar *to walk*
el camino *way, path, route*
el camión *bus (Mex)*
la camisa *shirt*
cancelar *to cancel*
la canción *song*
cantar *to sing*
el capitán *head waiter, maître (Mex)*
el cargo *charge*
cariñoso/a *affectionate*
el carnaval *carnival*
la carne *meat*
caro/a *dear*
la casa *house*
casi *almost*
el catálogo *catalogue*
catorce *fourteen*
la cebolla *onion*
cenar *to dine, have dinner*
la central (*road-transport*) *station (Mex)*
la central camionera *bus/coach station (Mex)*
el centro *centre*
la cerámica *ceramics, pottery*

cerca (de) near (to), close
cercano/a nearby
cero zero
cerquita near
cerrado/a closed
cerrar(ie) to close
la cerveza beer
el ceviche marinated raw fish
cien, ciento hundred
científico/a scientific
cierto certain, true
cinco five
cincuenta fifty
el cine cinema
el cinturón belt
el cinturón de seguridad seat belt
la cita appointment
la ciudad city, town
claro/a light
la clase class
el clóset (Mex) cupboard
cobrar to charge
la cocina kitchen; cuisine
el cóctel cocktail
el coche car
el cofre bonnet (Mex)
el colectivo minibus taxi
el/la colega colleague
colgar to hang-up (phone)
la colonia district (Mex)
el color colour
comer to eat; have lunch
cómico/a comic, funny
¿cómo? how?
como like; as
cómodo/a comfortable
compartir to divide up, share out
comprar to buy
comprender to understand
el compromiso date, engagement
comunicar to speak (phone)
comunitario/a community
con with
conceder to concede, grant
el concierto concert
el conmutador switch-board (Mex)
conocer* to know

conservar to preserve
considerar to consider
el consultorio consulting room; surgery
el contacto contact
contento/a happy
contestar to answer
convenir(ie) to suit, be convenient
coralino/a coral
el corazón heart
Correos Post Office
correr to run
la correspondencia connection
la cosa thing
la costa coast
costar (ue) to cost
crecer to grow
el crédito credit
creer to believe, think
la crema cream; café con crema white coffee
la crepa (Mex) pancake, crêpe
cruzar to cross
la cuadra block (Mex)
¿cuál? which?, what?
cualquier(a) any
en cuanto as soon as
¿cuánto? how much?
cuarenta forty
el cuate (Mex) friend
cuatro four
cuidarse to take care of oneself
la cultura culture
cultural cultural
el cumpleaños birthday
el curso course

CH

la charreada (Mex) rodeo
la charrería (Mex) horsemanship
el charro (Mex) cowboy, horseman
checar (Mex) to check
el cheque cheque
el chile chilli
chiquito/a little
el chocolate chocolate

D

la danza *dance*
el dato *fact*
  dar *to give*
  deber *to owe*
  decir* *to say, tell*
  definitivamente *definitely*
  delante *in front, before*
  delgado/a *thin*
  demasiado *too; too much*
  demográfico/a *demographic*
  demorarse *to be delayed*
el departamento *apartment* (*Mex*)
  depender (ie) (de) *to depend* (*on*)
el/la dependiente/a *employee; shop assistant*
  deportivo/a *sports*
  depositar *to deposit*
el depósito *deposit*
la derecha *right*
  derechito *straight on*
  derivar *to derive*
  desayunar *to have breakfast*
  descansar *to rest, relax*
el descanso *rest*
  descompuesto/a *broken (car)* (*Mex*)
  desde *from, since;* desde luego *of course*
  desear *to want, wish*
  desempacar (*Mex*) *to unpack*
  despacio *slow*
el despertador *alarm*
  despertar (ie) *to wake*
  despertarse *to wake up*
  después *after*
el detalle *detail*
  detrás *behind*
  devolver (ue) *to return*
el día *day*
  diario/a *daily*
  diez *ten*
el dinero *money*
la dirección *address*
  directamente *directly*
  directo/a *direct*
el directorio *directory*
  disculpar *to forgive;* ¡discúlpeme! *excuse me*
la distancia *distance*
  divertido/a *amusing, fun*

  divertirse (ie) *to enjoy oneself, have fun*
  documentar *to check in (luggage)* (*Mex*)
el dólar *dollar*
  doler (ue) *to hurt*
el dolor *pain*
el domingo *Sunday*
  ¿dónde? *where?*
  donde *where*
  dormir (ue) *to sleep*
  dos *two*
  dramático/a *dramatic*
  dulce *sweet*
  durante *during*
  durar *to last*

E

  e = y (*before word beginning with* i *or* hi)
  económico/a *inexpensive*
  echar *to throw, cast* echar un vistazo *to have a look*
en efectivo *in cash*
el ejemplo *example*
  por ejemplo *for example*
el ejercicio *exercise*
los electrodomésticos *household electrical goods*
el elevador (*Mex*) *lift*
el elote (*Mex*) *sweet corn*
  empanizado/a (*Mex*) *fried in breadcrumbs*
el/la empleado/a *employee*
  en *in; on* en autobús *by coach*
  encantar *to like, love*
  encontrar (ue) *to meet*
la enchilada *enchilada – taco with sauce*
  enfrente (de) *opposite*
la ensalada *salad*
  entonces *then, so*
la entrada *entrance; ticket for performance*
  entre *among; between*
  entre semana *on weekdays*
la época *period*
el equipaje *luggage*
el equipaje de mano *hand luggage*
el equipo *equipment*
  equivocado/a *mistaken*
la escala *stopover*
la escalera *staircase*
  escribir *to write*
  escrito/a *written*

el/la escritor(a) *writer*
escuchar *to listen (to)*
la escuela *school*
el esnórkel *snorkel*
eso *that* eso (es) *that's right*
España *Spain*
español(a) *Spanish*
especial *special*
la especialidad *speciality*
esperar *to wait for; to hope*
la esquina *corner*
la estación *station*
el estado *state*
los Estados Unidos *United States*
estadounidense *from/of the U.S.*
la estampilla *postage stamp (Mex)*
estar *to be*
este/a *this*
esto *this*
estrenar *to show for the first time*
el/la estudiante *student*
estudiar *to study*
la estufa *cooker (Mex)*
estupendo/a *great, stupendous*
el examen *exam*
excepcionalmente *exceptionally; just the once*
la excursión *excursion*
la excusa *excuse*
la experiencia *experience*
la explosión *explosion*
la expresión *expression*
exquisito/a *exquisite, delicious*
exterior *exterior*
extrañar *to miss (Mex)*
extraordinario/a *extraordinary*

F

la fábrica *factory*
fácil *easy*
la facultad *faculty*
faltar *to be missing, lacking*
la fama *fame; reputation*
la familia *family*
famoso/a *famous*
fanático/a *fanatic*
fascinado/a *fascinated*
por favor *please*

la fecha *date*
feo/a *ugly*
la feria *fair, festival*
la fiesta *festival; party*
fijarse *to notice, pay attention*
¡fíjate! *just fancy!*
fijo/a *fixed*
el filete *fillet*
la filosofía *philosophy*
el fin *end*
el fin de semana *weekend*
el final *end*
firmar *to sign*
físicamente *physically*
la flor *flower*
florido/a *flowery*
folklórico/a *popular, traditional*
el folleto *leaflet*
la forma *form (Mex)*
fornido/a *strong, well-built*
francamente *frankly*
el francés *French*
la frase *phrase, sentence*
fresco/a *fresh; cool*
el frijol *bean*
frijoles refritos *(Mex) purée of black beans*
frito/a *fried*
la frontera *frontier*
la fruta *fruit*
fuerte *strong*
fumar *to smoke*
funcionar *to work*
el fundamento *foundation*
el fútbol *football*
el futuro *future*

G

la gana *wish*
tener ganas de *to feel like*
el garaje *garage*
en general *in general*
generalmente *generally*
la gente *people*
la geografía *geography*
el/la gerente *manager*
el gimnasio *gymnasium*
la gloria *glory*

la glorieta *roundabout*
golpear *to hit*
gordo/a *fat*
gracias *thank you*
grande *big*
gringo/a (*Mex coll*) *person from the U.S.*
el grito *shout*
el grupo *group*
el guacamole *avocado purée*
guapo/a *attractive, good-looking*
la guayabera (*Mex*) *shirt*
güero/a (*Mex*) *fair (of hair or skin)*
la guitarra *guitar*
gustar *to please*
el gusto *taste; pleasure*
mucho gusto *pleased to meet you*

H

la habitación *room*
el habitante *inhabitant*
hablar *to speak*
hacer* *to do, make*
el hambre *hunger* tener hambre *to be hungry*
la hamburguesa *hamburger*
hasta *as far as, up to; not until* (*Mex*)
hasta luego *see you soon; goodbye*
hay *there is/are*
el/la hermano/a *brother/sister*
hermoso/a *lovely, beautiful*
el/la hijo/a *son/daughter*
la historia *history*
histórico/a *historic*
la hojalatería *tin-ware*
¡hola! *hello*
el hombre *man*
honorable *honourable*
la hora *hour; time*
el horario *timetable*
el horno *oven*
el horror *horror*
¡qué horror! *how awful!*
los hot cakes (*Mex*) (*Scotch*) *pancakes*
hoy *today*
el huachinango (*Mex*) *red snapper*
el huésped *guest*
el huevo *egg*
el huipil (*Mex*) *embroidered smock*

el huitlacoche (*Mex*) *edible black fungus*

I

(de) ida *single, one way* ida y vuelta *return*
ideal *ideal*
la identificación *identification*
la iglesia *church*
ilimitado/a *unlimited*
la imagen *image*
la importancia *importance*
importar *to matter, be of importance*
el impuesto *tax*
incluido/a *included*
incrementar *to increase*
indígena *native, indigenous*
la influencia *influence*
la información *information*
inglés/inglesa *English*
inseparable *inseparable*
la instrucción *instruction*
el instrumento *instrument*
el/la insurgente *insurgent, rebel*
inteligente *intelligent*
interesante *interesting*
interesar *to interest*
introducido/a *introduced*
invitar *to invite*
ir* *to go*
irreal *unreal*
el italiano *Italian*
la izquierda *left*

J

jamás *never*
el jardín *garden*
jarocho/a (*Mex*) *from Veracruz*
el jitomate (*Mex*) *tomato*
el/la joven *young man/woman*
el juego *game*
el jugo *juice*
junto/a *together*

K

el kilometraje ilimitado *unlimited mileage*
el kilómetro *kilometre*

L

la *the (f); her; it (f)*
la laca *lacquer*
al lado (de) *beside, next to*
la lana *wool*
largo/a *long*
la lástima *shame, pity*
¡qué lástima! *what a shame!*
la lavandería *laundry*
lavar *to wash*
le *you, to you (formal sing.); him, to him;
    her, to her*
la lectura *reading*
la leche *milk*
la lechuga *lettuce*
lejano/a *distant*
lejos *far*
la lengua *language*
lento/a *slow*
Letras *Letters*
levantarse *to get up*
la ley *law*
libre *free*
la librería *bookshop*
el libro *book*
la licencia *licence*
Licenciado/a *see page 16*
limpiar *to clean*
la limpieza *cleaning*
limpio/a *clean*
lindo/a *sweet, nice; pretty*
la línea *line*
listo/a *ready*
lo *him; it (masculine)*
luego *then*
hasta luego *see you soon, goodbye*
el lugar *place*
el lunes *Monday*
la luz *light*

LL

la llamada *call*
llamar *to call*
la llanta *tyre*
llegar *to reach, get to*
llenar *to fill (in)*
lleno/a *full*
llevar *to carry, take*
llover(ue) *to rain*
la lluvia *rain*

M

la machaca (Mex) *dried beef*
mágico/a *magic*
magnífico/a *magnificent*
el maíz *maize*
mal *badly; with difficulty*
malo/a *bad*
la maleta *suitcase*
mandar *to send; order*
¿mande? *pardon? (Mex)*
manejar *to drive (Mex)*
la manera *manner*
el mango *mango*
la mano *hand*
la mansión *mansion*
la mantequilla *butter*
mañana *tomorrow*
la mañana *morning*
marcar *to dial*
la margarita *margarita – tequila cocktail*
el mariachi (Mex) *mariachi – traditional Mexican music*
la marimba *marimba*
el marisco *seafood*
el martes *Tuesday*
más *more; plus*
la máscara *mask*
mayo *May*
mayor *older*
me *me, to me; reflexive pronoun, see page 36*
mecánico/a *mechanical*
el/la mecánico *mechanic*
el/la médico *doctor*
el medio *middle*
mejor *better*
el melón *melon*
menor *younger*
menos *less; minus*
merecer *to merit, be worth*
merece la pena *it's worth it/the bother*
el mes *month*
la mesa *table*
mestizo/a *half-caste; (Mex) mixture of Spanish and
    indigenous Mexican blood*

meter *to put*
mexicano/a *Mexican*
mi *my*
mí *me*
la miel *honey; syrup* (*Mex*)
mientras *while*
el miércoles *Wednesday*
mil *thousand*
el milagro *miracle*
el millón *million*
el minuto *minute*
mirar *to look (at)*
mismo/a *same*
moderno/a *modern*
el mole (*Mex*) *mole – a sauce*
molestar *to bother*
el momento *moment*
la moneda *change; coin*
el monstruo *monster*
moreno/a *dark (of hair or skin)*
el moro *Moor*
la mostaza *mustard*
el motor *engine*
el/la muchacho/a *boy/girl*
mucho/a *much, a lot*
el mueble *piece of furniture*
muerto/a *dead*
la mujer *woman*
el mundo *world*
el museo *museum*
la música *music*
musical *musical*
muy *very*

N

nada *nothing*
nadar *to swim*
nadie *no one*
necesario/a *necessary*
necesitar *to need*
ni *not even* ni . . . ni *neither . . . nor*
ningún/ninguno/a *no*
no *no, not*
la noche *night* buenas noches *good evening/night*
el norte *north*
norteamericano/a *North American; from the U.S.*
norteño/a *northern*

nos *us, to us; reflexive pronoun, see page 36*
nosotros *we*
la nota: la nota de consumo *receipt*
noticiero/a *news*
noventa *ninety*
nuestro/a *our*
nueve *nine*
nuevo/a *new*
el número *number*
nunca *never*

O

o *or*
la obra *work*
el obstáculo *obstacle*
ocupado/a *busy*
ocho *eight*
la oficina *office*
ofrecer *to offer*
oir *to hear*
¡ojalá! *if only it were so!*
la olla *pot*
opinar *to think*
la opinión *opinion*
la óptica *optician*
la orden *portion* (*Mex*)
a sus órdenes *can I help you?* (*Mex*)
la orfebrería *metal-work*
original *original*
el oro *gold*
oro negro *black gold (i.e. oil)*
oscuro/a *dark*
el ostión (*Mex*) *oyster*
otro/a *other*

P

padre *great* (*Mex*)
el padre *father*
pagar *to pay*
el país *country*
la palabra *word*
el pan *bread*
el pan tostado *toast*
la papa (*Mex*) *potato*
las papas francesas (*Mex*) *chips*
el papá *father*
la papaya *paw-paw*

para *for, in order to*
la parada *stop*
parecer *to seem*
la pareja *couple; partner*
el parque *park*
la parrilla *grill*
a la parrilla *grilled*
la parte *part*
de parte de *from, on behalf of*
el pasado *past*
el/la pasajero/a *passenger*
el pasaporte *passport*
pasar *to pass, go to*
pasar por *to pick up*
el paseo *walk; avenue*
el pasillo *corridor, gangway*
la pasión *passion*
el paso *step*
la patria *country*
el patrón/la patrona *patron*
la película *film*
la pelota *ball*
la peluquería *hairdresser*
la pena *sorrow; trouble* merece la pena *it's worth the trouble* ¡qué pena! *what a shame!*
pensar (ie) *to think*
peor *worse*
pequeño/a *small*
perder *to lose*
perdón *pardon, excuse me*
perfecto/a *perfect*
permanecer *to remain, stay*
permitir *to allow*
pero *but*
la persona *person*
personal *personal*
pesado/a *heavy*
pesar *to weigh*
el pescado *fish*
el pesero (Mex) *minibus taxi*
el peso *peso – Mexican unit of currency*
el petróleo *oil, petroleum*
el pez *fish*
picante *hot, spicy*
a pie *on foot*
la pila *battery*
el/la pintor(a) *painter*

la piña *pineapple*
la pirámide *pyramid*
el piso *floor*
planchar *to iron*
planetario/a *planetary*
el plano *plan*
el plástico *plastic*
la plata *silver*
el plátano *banana*
platicar *to chat (Mex)*
el plato *dish*
la playa *beach*
poblano/a *from Puebla*
un poco *a little*
poco/a *little, few*
poder (ue)* *to be able, can*
policíaco/a *thriller*
el pollo *chicken*
ponchado/a *punctured, flat (Mex)*
poner* *to put*
popular *popular*
por *by; along, through; for; per*
porque *because*
¿por qué? *why?*
posible *possible*
el postre *pudding, dessert*
el pozole *stew (Mex)*
practicar *to play (a sport)*
el precio *price*
precioso/a *lovely; precious*
precisamente *precisely*
preferir (ie) *to prefer*
preguntar *to ask*
preocuparse *to worry*
la presentación *presentation*
presentarse *to report, show oneself*
el presente *present*
el presidente *president*
la primavera *spring*
primero/a *first*
el/la primo/a *cousin*
principal *principal, main*
el/la principiante *beginner*
el problema *problem*
el producto *product*
el programa *programme*
pronunciar *to pronounce*

la propina *tip*
próximo/a *next*
la publicación *publication*
el pueblo *town, village*
la puerta *gate, door*
pues *then, so, well*
la pupila *pupil (of eye)*

Q

que *which, that*
¿qué? *what?*
quedar *to remain, be left*
querer (ie) *to want; to love*
quien *who*
¿quién? *who?*
quince *fifteen*
quinientos *five hundred*
quizás *perhaps*

R

la radio *radio*
ranchero/a *ranch*
rápido/a *fast*
el rato *moment*
la raza *race*
la razón *reason* tener razón *to be right*
realmente *really*
el rebozo *shawl*
el recado *message*
la recámara (*Mex*) *bedroom*
el/la recepcionista *receptionist*
recibir *to receive*
recoger *to collect, pick up*
recomendar (ie) *to recommend*
reconocer* *to recognise*
el refresco *soft drink*
el refrigerador (*Mex*) *fridge*
la regadera *shower (Mex)*
registrarse *to register*
regresar *to return*
la reina *queen*
relajante *relaxing*
la relojería *watch (repair) shop*
rentar (*Mex*) *to rent, hire*
reparar *to repair*
repetir *to repeat*

la res: la carne de res (*Mex*) *beef*
la reservación *reservation*
reservar *to reserve*
el restaurante *restaurant*
el restorán (*Mex*) *restaurant*
el retraso *delay*
revisar *to have a look at, check over*
revuelto: huevos revueltos *scrambled eggs*
el rey *king*
el rincón *corner*
rogar (ue) *to request*
rojo/a *red*
la ropa *clothes*
roto/a *broken*
rubio/a *fair (of hair or skin)*
el ruido *noise*

S

el sábado *Saturday*
saber* *to know*
la sala *room*
la salida *departure*
saliendo *leaving*
salir *to leave, go out*
el salón: el salón de baile *dance-hall*
la salsa *sauce*
el saludo *greeting*
la sandía *water melon*
el sarape (*Mex*) *blanket*
se *(pronoun, see page 49)*
la sección *section*
el/la secretario/a *secretary*
la sed *thirst* tener sed *to be thirsty*
en seguida *straight away*
seguir (i) *to follow*
segundo/a *second*
seguro/a *sure, certain*
el seguro *insurance cover*
seis *six*
la selva *jungle*
el semáforo *traffic light*
la semana *week*
sentar (ie) *to feel; be sorry* lo siento *I'm sorry*
sentarse (ie) *to sit*
el/la señor(a) *Mr., Mrs.*
separado/a *separate*
septiembre *September*

ser* *to be*
el servicio *service*
servir (i) *to serve*
para servirle *you're welcome*
sesenta *sixty*
setenta *seventy*
sí *yes*
si *if, whether*
el sidral (*Mex*) *apple drink*
siempre *always*
siendo *being*
el siglo *century*
significar *to mean*
siguiente *following, next*
simpático/a *nice, friendly*
sin *without*
sino *but*
el sitio *place, site*
sobre *on, about*
la sociedad *society*
el sol *sun*
solicitar *to ask for*
solo/a *alone*
sólo *only*
el/la soltero/a *single, unmarried*
el son *type of music*
el sonido *sound*
la sopa *soup*
su, sus *your; his, her, its; their*
la subida *ascent*
subirse a *to get into*
sudamericano/a *South American*
sugerir (ie) *to suggest*
la suite *self-catering, service flat (Mex)*
el supermercado *supermarket*
el súper *supermarket*
suponer* *to suppose*
por supuesto *of course*

T

el taco *a filled tortilla (Mex)*
el taller *workshop; repair garage*
el tamal (*Mex*) *dumpling*
también *also, too, as well*
tampoco *neither*
tan *so*
el tanque *cylinder*

tanto/a *so much*
tapatío/a (*Mex*) *from Jalisco*
el tapete *rug*
la taquilla *kiosk, booth*
tardar *to take (of time)*
la tarde *afternoon, evening*
la tarea *homework; task*
la tarjeta *card* la tarjeta de abordar (*Mex*) *boarding card*
el taxi *taxi*
el taxímetro *taxi meter*
el/la taxista *taxi driver*
te *you, to you; reflexive pronoun, see page 36*
el teatro *theatre*
la tele *telly*
el teléfono *telephone*
la telenovela *television soap opera*
la televisión *television*
la temporada *season*
temprano *early*
tener* *to have*
tener ganas de *to feel like*
tener hambre *to be hungry*
tener que (*+ infinitive*) *to have to*
tener razón *to be right*
tener sed *to be thirsty*
la tequila (*Mex*) *tequila – alcoholic drink made from cactus*
la terraza *terrace*
ti *(to) you*
el tiempo *time; weather*
la tierra *earth; land*
la tina *bath*
la tintorería *dry cleaner's*
típico/a *typical*
el tipo de cambio *exchange note*
tocar *to play*
el tocino *bacon*
todavía *still*
todo *all, everything* sobre todo *above all*
todo/a *all, every*
tomar *to take; to have (a drink)* tomar el sol *to sunbathe*
el tono *tone*
la toronja (*Mex*) *grapefruit*
la tortilla *maize pancake (Mex)*
tostado/a *toasted*

trabajar *to work*
el trabajo *work*
tradicional *traditional*
traer* *to bring, carry*
el tráfico *traffic*
tranquilizarse *to calm down*
tranquilo/a *quiet*
el/la transeúnte *passer-by*
el tránsito *traffic*
el transporte *transport*
treinta *thirty*
el tren *train*
tres *three*
el trigo *corn*
trigueño/a *fair (of skin or hair)*
triste *sad*
la trompeta *trumpet*
el trono *throne*
tropical *tropical*
tu *your (familiar)*
tú *you (familiar)*
el turismo *tourism*
el/la turista *tourist*
turístico/a *tourist*

U

últimamente *recently*
último/a *last*
un(a) *a, one*
único/a *only*
uno *one*
unos *some*
usted *you (formal)*
ustedes *you (pl – formal and informal (Mex))*
utilizar *to use*

V

las vacaciones *holidays*
la vajilla *crockery, china*

el valle *valley*
a veces *sometimes*
venir* *to come*
la venta *sale*
la ventanilla *window*
ver *to see*
veracruzano/a *from, of Veracruz*
la verdad *truth*
verde *green*
la verdura *greenery*
las verduras mixtas *mixed vegetables*
la vez *time* otra vez *again*
viajar *to travel*
el/la viajero/a *traveller*
el video *video*
el viernes *Friday*
el violín *violin*
visitar *to visit*
el visor *mask*
el vistazo *a look* echar un vistazo *to have a look*
vivir *to live*
volver (ue) *to return*
vosotros *you (plural, informal; NOT Mex)*
la voz *voice*
el vuelo *flight*
la vuelta *return*

Y

y *and*
ya *already, now*
yo *I*

Z

la zanahoria *carrot*
la zapatería *shoe (repair) shop*
el zapato *shoe*
zapoteca *Zapotec*
la zona *zone, area*

Learn another language with the BBC

The following are available from good bookshops:

French

A Vous La France:	First stage book
	Cassette 1
	Cassette 2
	Teacher's notes
	Language pack (book and cassettes)
	Language file workbook
France Extra:	Second stage book
	Cassette pack
	Teacher's notes
Franc-Parler:	Third stage book
	Cassette pack

German

Deutsch Direkt:	First stage book
	Cassette 1
	Cassette 2
	Tutor's notes
	Language pack (book and cassettes)
	Language file workbook
Deutsch Express:	Second stage book
	Teacher's notes
	Cassette pack
Ganz Spontan:	Third stage book
	Cassette pack

Greek

Greek Language and People:	Book
	Cassette pack

Hindi Urdu

Hindi Urdu Bol	
Chaal:	Book
	Cassette

Italian

Buongiorno Italia:	First stage book
	Cassette 1
	Cassette 2
	Cassette 3
	Teacher's notes
	Language pack (book and cassettes)
	Language file workbook
L'Italia dal Vivo:	Second stage book
	Cassette pack

Portuguese

Discovering	
Portuguese:	Book
	Cassette pack
Russian Language	
and People:	Book
	Cassette pack

Spanish

Espana Viva:	First stage book
	Cassette 1
	Cassette 2
	Language pack (book and cassettes)
	Language file workbook
Paso Doble:	Second stage book
	Cassette pack

For business travellers and holidaymakers the Get By
series features the following titles:

Get By in:
              Arabic book
              Arabic cassette pack
              Chinese book
              Chinese cassette pack
              French book
              French cassette pack
              German book
              German cassette pack
              Greek book
              Greek cassette pack
              Hindu Urdu book
              Hindi Urdu cassette pack
              Italian book
              Italian cassette pack
              Japanese book
              Japanese cassette pack
              Portuguese book
              Portuguese cassette pack
              Spanish book
              Spanish cassette pack
              Turkish book
              Turkish cassette pack

Also useful for holidaymakers are the following titles:

When in France:
              Book
              Cassette

When in Italy:
              Book
              Cassette

When in Italy:
              Book
              Cassette